ALLIES

Why the West Had to
Remove Saddam

WILLIAM SHAWCROSS

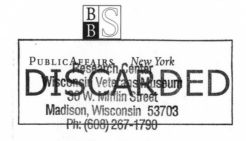

PUBLICAFFAIRS New York

*To my much loved
and much missed parents,
Hartley and Joan.*

Book design by Mark McGarry
Set in Dante

Library of Congress Cataloging-in-Publication Data
Shawcross, William
Allies: The U.S., Britain, Europe, and the War in Iraq / by William Shawcross.
p. cm.
Includes bibliographical references and index.
ISBN-13 978-1-58648-347-0
ISBN 1-58648-347-1
1. Iraq War, 2003. 2. Europe—Foreign relations—United States. 3. United
States—Foreign relations—Europe. 4. United States—Foreign relations—2001–
I. Title
D279.76.S53 2004   956.7044'3--dc22   2003064786

10 9 8 7 6 5 4 3 2 1

CONTENTS

INTRODUCTION

O N AUGUST 19, 2003, a truck filled with explosives was driven into the Canal Hotel, the United Nations head-quarters in Baghdad. The building contained the offices of 300 international and Iraqi civil servants and humanitarian workers. The bomb was targeted directly at the office of UN Secretary-General Special Representative Sergio Vieira de Mello.

This was the international version of September 11. 9/11 was an attack against America; 8/19 was an attack, by the same sort of people, against the international system.

The bomber killed more than twenty people, including UN officials, and wounded scores of others. This number is not to be compared with those who died on September 11, but the impact is enormous. The terrorists who carried out this attack murdered more UN officials in any single assault since the organization was created following World War II. It represented a direct assault against the principles of international civil society that the world has tried to create since 1945. It was an attempt to murder not only fine men and women but also all the humane values that the UN, for all its shortcomings, represents and strives to fulfill.

Sergio Vieira de Mello was one of the most brilliant diplomats at the United Nations. He was considered to be a possible successor to Kofi Annan as Secretary-General, and it would have been a great appointment. On his death, Brazil, his home country, at once announced three days of official mourning.

His working life covered the gamut of the world's attempts to deal with evil and its aftermath. After joining the Office of the United Nations High Commissioner for Refugees, he had worked in the 1970s in Bangladesh, in southern Sudan, in Mozambique, in Latin America, and in Lebanon. Later he moved to Indochina to help first with the Vietnamese boatpeople and then in Cambodia. Everywhere he worked with the same mix of dedication and flair.

I had known Sergio for many years, and I had watched him work in Cambodia, in the Balkans, in East Timor, and in Africa. He was a joy to be with—a magnetic personality. He spoke at least five languages fluently.

In Cambodia in the early 1990s, he was in charge of the

repatriation of several hundred thousand refugees. He dealt with the odious Khmer Rouge commanders and with the intransigent officials of the communist regime in Phnom Penh with equal charm, firmness, clarity, and skill. He made all the arrangements meticulously, and for an operation of that scale the repatriation was pretty flawless.

In Bosnia he slept and worked in one room in the head-quarters of the UN Force Commander. I remember going with him to meet the egregious Bosnian Serb leader, Radovan Karadzic, in Pale. Karadzic was a psychiatrist of sorts, and Sergio gave him the latest edition of the *New York Review of Books*, in which a cover story was about war between psychiatrists. Having charmed Karadzic, Sergio then sat down to hours of tough negotiations with him.

He was intensely serious about his work, but he could also laugh and make fun of himself and the predicaments in which he often landed. He was debonair, immaculately dressed, remarkably handsome, carrying a smile that could launch a thousand cease-fires. Women adored him. Men admired him. One U.S. senator once said, "Whenever I meet Sergio, two things happen. First, I feel poorly in-formed and secondly, I feel poorly dressed." I have never heard anyone speak unkindly of him. People talked of "Sergio's magic."

We used to joke that the only possible title for his eventual memoir was "My Friends—The War Criminals." Now he will never get to write it because the war criminals got him.

In 1999 Kofi Annan had asked him to go to East Timor after the Indonesians had finally been compelled to leave after their brutal twenty-five-year occupation. Vieira de Mello helped lead the tiny society out of the wreckage left by Indonesia and into full independence, restoring its utilities and creating the foundations of civil society.

For this he and the UN were denounced by Osama bin Laden. Why? Because the UN had helped a basically Christian community secure its freedom from its Muslim occupiers.

Since then Annan had appointed him UN High Commissioner for Human Rights, a difficult job that he was just settling into at the time of the invasion of Iraq in spring 2003.

After the fall of Saddam Hussein's regime, the UN Security Council passed Resolution 1483 acknowledging the U.S.-led occupation of Iraq. Annan asked Vieira de Mello to go to Baghdad for just four months to set up an assistance mission. He was not very keen on the idea, but he understood the opportunities for Iraq as well as the dangers for himself and others.

His friend, the Peruvian novelist Mario Vargas Llosa, visited him in Baghdad and asked him, "Aren't you tired of so many horrors? Why did you agree to come to this place?"

"I found no good arguments for refusing," Sergio replied, "with his eternal ear-to-ear smile."

Sergio saw that the UN role was to lay the foundations of civil society in a country terrorized by decades of brutal dictatorship. He said, "The people of Iraq have suffered enough. It is time that we all... come together to ensure that this suffering comes to an end.... We must not fail." He quickly won the confidence of Paul Bremer, the U.S. administrator, and argued that the Iraqis must be empowered as quickly as possible. He spent his time meeting and talking to people and organizations from all parts of Iraqi society and traveling the region, trying to persuade the neighboring governments to give the new Iraq a chance.

He learned enough Arabic to charm Iraqis in their own language and was in every way a very good friend to them. That was one reason why the terrorists killed him and many of the well-chosen team of UN officials assisting him. They included Sergio's chief of staff, the Egyptian diplomat Nadia Younes, who was a delightful iconoclast with a deep-throated and constant laugh, as well as one of Kofi Annan's most trusted lieutenants, and dedicated young people including Rick Hooper, an American, Fiona Watson (British), and Ranillo Buenaventura (Filipino), along with many others.

It was not clear whether the murderers were Baathist

remnants of the Saddam regime or Islamic fundamentalists who had in recent weeks been rushing to Iraq to create a new war against the "crusaders." There were suggestions that the two groups might have collaborated for this operation. Whoever they are, they were determined to stop the international community from building a decent Iraq. They wanted despotism—either Baathist or Islamic—to prevail. They had no thought for the welfare of the Iraqi people whom the UN was attempting to assist.

A few days after the attack, a communiqué published by Al Qaeda described the bombing thus: "One of the Mujahedeen broke in with a van full of explosives into the back part of the headquarters at the office of the personal representative of America's criminal slave, Kofi Annan, the diseased Sergio de Mello, criminal Bush's friend." The statement asked: "Why cry over a heretic...? Sergio Vieira De Mello is the one who tried to embellish the image of America, the crusaders and the Jews in Lebanon and Kosovo, and now in Iraq. He is America's first man where he was nominated by Bush to be in charge of the UN after Kofi Annan, the criminal and slave of America; and he is the crusader that extracted a part of the Islamic land [East Timor]."

Whether the murderers were inspired by Al Qaeda or were Baathists, they are people determined to destroy the international system we have slowly tried to build since 1945.

Mario Vargas Llosa was right when he wrote,

> The attack was perpetrated by one of various sects and movements bent on provoking the Apocalypse in order to prevent Iraq from soon becoming a free and modern country ruled by democratic laws and representative governments, a perspective that rightfully terrifies and drives insane the gangs of murderers and torturers of the Mukhbarat and the Fedayeen of Saddam Hussein along with the fundamentalist commandos from Al Qaeda and Ansar al Islam as well as the terrorist brigades sent to Iraq by the ultra conservative Iranian clerics. All of them, totalling only a few thousand armed fanatics, but with extraordinary tools for destruction, know that if Iraq becomes a modern democracy, their days are numbered.

This book is not a narrative of the war in Iraq but a glance at one of the ways in which the international community, following 9/11, confronted evil. The nature of the threat to global security was now seen to be different to any posed before. Decisionmaking becomes more difficult and more tragic in a world threatened as never before by terrorism and the proliferation of weapons of mass destruction (WMD).

It has placed unprecedented stress upon the machinery

of international cooperation and diplomacy. It has caused old friends to disagree bitterly, and it has uncovered inconsistency and hypocrisy in many nations' foreign policies.

In a sense this book takes up some of the themes I tried to discuss in my 2000 book *Deliver Us from Evil*. How can the international community best deal with tyrants, rogue states, and terrorists who threaten not only their own people but also others—and who defy the world's attempts to restrain them?

Since 9/11 those questions have become even more important, even more difficult to answer. The risk to everyone engaged in dealing with evil is exemplified in the brutal destruction of those fine people in the Canal Hotel. It is symbolic of a wider risk to all nations and to the alliances that bind the international community—alliances that since 1945 have created the institutions that have advanced democratic civil societies around the world.

Iraq is at the center of the mission to face down fundamentalist malevolence and reactionary despotism. The nature of the battle was well described by Bahram Saleh, the prime minister of the Kurdish-controlled zone of northern Iraq. "Iraq is the nexus where many issues are coming together—Islam versus democracy, the West versus the axis of evil, Arab nationalism versus some different types of political culture," he told the *New York Times*. "If the Americans succeed here, this will be a monumental blow to everything the terrorists stand for."

The corollary of that is very simple. If the U.S.-UK-led effort to create a better system of government in Iraq fails, the men who carried out 9/11 and 8/19 will have won a terrible victory. The consequences for the world do not bear consideration.

London
November 2003

Chapter 1

THE GATE OF FIRE

We entered the twenty-first century through a gate of fire.

KOFI ANNAN

T HIS EVOCATIVE and chastening description of September 11 was given by the UN Secretary-General in December 2001 as he accepted the Nobel Prize for Peace personally and on behalf of the entire UN organization.

That gate of fire was awful, but not unexpected. For years terrorist threats had been made, and many had been carried out. There had been warnings, not just from intelligence agencies, of even worse to come.

In November 1998 Peggy Noonan, speechwriter to President Ronald Reagan, wrote,

> We live in a world of three billion men and hundreds of thousands of nuclear bombs, missiles, warheads: it's a world of extraordinary germs that can be harnessed and used to kill whole populations, a world of extraordinary

chemicals that can be harnessed and used to do the same.... Three billion men and it takes only half a dozen bright and evil ones to harness and deploy. What are the odds it will happen? Put it another way: what are the odds it will not? Low. Non-existent, I think.

When you consider who is gifted and crazed with rage... when you think of the terrorist places and the terrorist countries... who do they hate the most? The Great Satan, the United States. What is its most important place? Some would say Washington. I would say the great city of the United States is the great city of the world, the dense, ten mile long island called Manhattan, where the economic and media power of the nation resides, the city that is the psychological centre of our modernity, our hedonism, our creativity, our hard shouldered hipness, our unthinking arrogance.

On September 11, 2001, it happened. In George Bush's words that evening, night fell on a different world.

The lessons of Vietnam, which since the 1970s had replaced the lessons of Munich and held U.S. policymakers and soldiers in thrall, vanished instantly. By September 12 the only lessons that mattered were those of 9/11 itself, and they were not instantly easy to comprehend.

It is impossible to overemphasize the importance of that

day's attacks. The last time something comparable happened on American soil was when the British burned the White House in August 1814. For Americans it made a new world, if not a new America. Yet some say that America just became more itself. Because America is the dominating power in the world, much that is happening today is the result of September 11. The republic was transformed, and the world's polity with it.

In his Nobel speech, Kofi Annan emphasized the global nature of the new situation: "New threats make no distinction between races, nations or regions. A new insecurity has entered every mind, regardless of wealth or status.... This new reality can no longer be ignored. It must be confronted." He was right. It is impossible to pass back through that gate. But the hardest task is now to determine the most effective way to confront the new, deadly, all-pervasive threat.

Annan's words found an echo in those of the outgoing secretary-general of NATO, George Robertson: "A special breed of terrorism has come to the fore—driven not by achievable political aims, but by fanatical extremism and the urge to kill." Robertson continued with an image, not of a gate of fire, but borrowed from an old tale from the Middle East. "It is difficult," he said, "to imagine how one could return this cruel genie to its pre-9/11 bottle."

Difficult? It is almost certainly *impossible*. When Western intelligence agents were able to examine Al Qaeda training camps in Afghanistan, they were alarmed to discover that the terrorists were far more advanced in the creation of so-called dirty bombs (i.e., crude radiological, chemical or biological weapons) than they had realized. Eliza Manningham-Buller, the head of MI5, the British intelligence agency, later warned that an attack against a major Western city with even a rudimentary radioactive, biological, or chemical weapon was "only a matter of time."

She said that intelligence reports showed that "renegade scientists" had given terrorist groups the information they needed to create such weapons. "My conclusion, based on the intelligence we have received, is that we are faced with a realistic possibility of some form of unconventional attack that could include chemical, biological, radioactive, or nuclear attack."

She warned also that the task of containing Al Qaeda was difficult because it operated on a global scale and was impervious to political dialogue. "If this is a war that can be won, it is not going to be won soon. The supply of potential terrorists among extreme elements is unlikely to diminish. Breaking the link between terrorism and religious ideology is difficult in the short term." It is all the more difficult because of the failure of the Arab world—though not the entire Islamic world—to adapt to the twentieth century let alone the twenty-first.

Distorting Islam, ideologues like Osama bin Laden insist that all the evils in the Islamic world follow from the abandonment of the divine heritage of Islam. And governments of the region, oppressive and ineffectual, have all too often resorted to blaming their failures on the world outside, especially the United States—from which many of them also derive much of their financial and military support. They tyrannize and oppress and try to divert the fury of their peoples outward. Political dialogue and reconciliation is not possible with groups that have aims that are absolute and nonnegotiable.

The United Nations Development Programme has drawn attention to the overarching failure of the region in its Arab Development Report of 2002. It makes grim reading. Over the past twenty years, growth in per capita income was lower in the Arab world than anywhere else except sub-Saharan Africa. If current trends persist it would take the average Arab 140 years to double his income; other regions will do that in less than ten years. Labor productivity is declining, real wages have fallen, poverty has grown. The gross domestic product of all the Arab countries combined in 1999 was less than that of Spain. One out of every five Arabs lives on less than $2 a day. Unemployment is already about 15 percent of the labor force and is expected to double by 2010. There is also "poverty of capabilities and poverty of opportunities." These have their roots in three deficits: freedom, women's empowerment, and knowledge.

The report found that out of the seven regions of the world, the Arab region had the least freedoms of all—fewer civil liberties, fewer political rights, and less free media. Women were stifled more completely in the Arab states than anywhere else; one in two Arab women can neither read nor write. Scientific expenditure is lower than anywhere else—investment in research and development is less than one-seventh of the world's average. The information technology revolution has barely touched Arabia—only 0.6 percent of the population uses the Internet, and only 1.2 percent have personal computers.

The report noted that very little of this will change until Arab countries somehow acquire decent governments and good governance. Political freedom and political representation must be freed up; public administration must be reformed; civil society must be liberated; the media must be freed.

Bernard Lewis, one of the great Western authorities on Islamic culture, argues cogently that the two dominant movements of the twentieth century, nationalism and socialism, have both been tried in the Islamic world, and both have failed. In some countries the combination has created something even worse: "The bastard offspring of both ideologies, National Socialism, still survives in a few states that have preserved the Nazi Fascist style of dictatorial government and indoctrination." None more so than the Iraq of Saddam Hussein.

The consequences are alarming. As Lewis puts it, "If the peoples of the Middle East continue on their present path, the suicide bomber may become a metaphor for the whole region, and there will be no escape from a downward spiral of hate and spite, rage and self-pity, poverty and oppression."

But of course one has also to take into account the fact that Western governments have for decades supported Middle East regimes that may brutalize and impoverish the mass of the people but nonetheless provide stable oil supplies. The paradox is uncomfortable, the dilemma acute.

This terrible sense of failure is occurring in an increasingly unstable world. The Cold War imposed a kind of stability, often cruel, in which each superpower supported its own clients. Now many of those clients have been cut free without any means of support. In the Caucasus, in Central Asia, in northern Africa, and in the Middle East huge political and economic changes are taking place. They could easily lead to convulsions that will spill over into North

America and Europe. There is a real risk that more states will fail and fragment into regions run by warlords who finance themselves through sales of drugs or guns or the new illegal growth industry—the smuggling of people.

In such a world, risks that we used to accept are intolerable. In particular, the covert manufacture or acquisition of weapons of mass destruction by states that defy the rule of law and the normal codes of conduct among sovereign powers has assumed a frightening urgency. Iraq, Iran, and North Korea are all such states. How can the rest of the world protect itself against them? That is the vital question. At the beginning of the twenty-first century, geography does not act as a shield.

It was their interpretation of this fundamental reality that led the United States, Britain, and their allies to deal with Saddam Hussein in 2003.

The challenge to the international community in 2003 derived from the great difficulty that the world has in dealing with a criminal state determined to defy international norms and rules.

Weapons of mass destruction are the greatest threat to mankind today. Biological weapons have often been called the poor dictator's atomic bomb. Few people had been more diligent in trying to acquire and use them than Saddam Hussein. The roots of the crisis of 2003 stretch back through the desert into the tolerance of tyranny and its marriage to weapons that can kill millions. The problem can be stated simply: Saddam Hussein had made clear over decades that the death of hundreds of thousands of Iraqis was of no consequence to him. The death of millions of Iranians was to be desired. What would inhibit him from killing millions of Americans or Europeans as well if and when he had the means? Nothing in his record.

After rising through the use of ruthless guile through the Baath Party apparatus, Saddam Hussein became president of Iraq in 1979. His idol was Joseph Stalin, and he quickly set about purging his enemies (real or imagined) in the Baath Party and in the Iraqi government. In one of his first acts, he convened a meeting of senior party members and had one of them confess to leading a Syrian-backed plot. Saddam then read out the names of fifty-four more coconspirators, all of them sitting in the hall. In front of the cameras, each was led or dragged away, and Saddam then ordered all those party officials who had not been named to take part in the firing squads that dispatched the "guilty." The nature of his rule was thus set.

Abroad one of his first acts was to invade Iran, which he hoped would be unable to defend itself in the chaos of the

Islamic revolution that had suffused it since January 1979.

At that time, Iran was seen as one of the greatest threats to the West. Ayatollah Ruhollah Khomeini had driven from power the Shah of Iran, on whom the United States had relied as an integral part of its defense of the Middle East oil fields, and established an expansionist theocratic rule in Teheran. In November 1979 militants seized the U.S. Embassy in Teheran, taking fifty-two Americans hostage, a crisis that lasted more than a year and ended soon after the inauguration of President Ronald Reagan in January 1981.

That was not the end of the story. Khomeini preached war against the United States and Israel, murdered his opponents at home and abroad, backed Islamic terrorist groups targeting Israel, and called for Islamic revolution throughout the region.

And so to Washington and its allies any attempt to curb the Ayatollah seemed to have some merit. Saddam's invasion of Iran was a military failure, and Iraqi troops became mired in a long and costly war in which both sides lost enormous numbers of troops. In 1982 Khomeini launched a counterattack. The prospect of an Iranian fundamentalist victory was so alarming to Washington that the Reagan administration decided to give limited intelligence assistance to Saddam Hussein, despite his appalling record. France, already much closer to Saddam, assisted him as well. Germany supplied Iraq with industrial complexes able to produce chemical and biological weapons. Washington and its allies turned a blind eye when Iraq used chemical weapons against first Iran and then, in 1988, against Kurdish rebels in northern Iraq.

Iraq had begun to try to create a biological weapons program in the 1970s—after it had signed the 1972 international convention that banned the development and production of such weapons. Throughout the 1980s it developed biological and chemical weapons. It later acknowledged that it had used more than 100,000 chemical munitions against Iran. Iraqi insisted repeatedly that these weapons had been essential in stopping Iran's human-wave attacks against Iraqi positions.

In March 1988 Saddam's troops attacked the Iraqi Kurdish town of Halabja, in revenge for what he considered Kurdish collaboration with Iran. At least 5,000 people were gassed to death and another 7,000 were dreadfully injured. The massacre at Halabja was repeated in other Kurdish villages; this is the first time since the Holocaust that a government is known to have gassed its own people.

The story of Halabja and the Kurds is of immense importance. If Saddam was prepared to use outlawed chemical weapons on Iraq's own citizens, how could he ever be trusted not to use them on others?

Saddam had gained nothing from the Iran-Iraq War, but he had ruined and bankrupted his country. The dreadful conflict had helped the West in that it slowed the Ayatollah's long arm of revolution. But Washington had failed to understand adequately the nature of the Iraqi devil with whom it was supping.

Then Saddam took an extraordinary risk. In August 1990, partly in order to secure its great oil wealth, he invaded Kuwait and announced its annexation as Iraq's nineteenth province. If that conquest had been allowed to stand, it would have created a precedent to be feared by all small sovereign nations. Moreover, Saddam would have controlled 9 percent of the world's oil production, almost as much as the Saudis, who themselves feared assault by their aggressive neighbor.

Washington finally understood the threat to stability that Saddam posed, with his regional ambitions, his merciless tyranny, and his dedicated pursuit of weapons of mass destruction. President George H. W. Bush and British Prime Minister Margaret Thatcher announced in Aspen, Colorado, the day after the invasion that it must not stand. The UN Security Council passed Resolution 678, which authorized the allies to expel Iraq from Kuwait and to use force in support of all "subsequent relevant resolutions needed to restore international peace and security" to the region. President Bush sent then–Defense Secretary Dick Cheney to Riyadh to persuade the Saudis to accept U.S. protection. He succeeded, and U.S. troops were immediately airlifted into the country. Saddam refused to accede to demands that he withdraw, and Washington and London began to build up troops and recruit the partners needed to drive Saddam from Kuwait.

On January 17, 1991, the U.S.-led Coalition launched Operation Desert Storm with a massive air offensive against Iraqi positions. The ground campaign was begun on February 24. Despite predictions of disaster from those who opposed the use of force against Iraq, Coalition forces immediately succeeded in destroying large Iraqi formations. Indeed, Saddam risked losing his entire army, in particular the Republican Guards on which his regime depended. On February 28, President Bush ordered a halt to the ground offensive. As a result many of Saddam's best troops escaped.

U.S. reluctance to complete the removal of Saddam seems in retrospect a terrible mistake, even if some of the reasons were understandable at the time. The UN mandate was for the liberation of Kuwait, not the overthrow of Saddam, and however much many of the Arab Coalition partners might have privately longed for his removal from their area, they dared not say so publicly, let alone cooperate in his overthrow. The UN system was already stretched to the limit by U.S. pressure. Moreover, there was widespread belief that Saddam, having suffered such a terrible defeat and such an extraordinary loss of face, would likely be overthrown from within.

Then another mistake. President Bush called upon "the Iraqi military and the Iraqi people to take matters into their own hands and force Saddam Hussein the dictator to step aside." Iraqis, particularly the Shiite majority always oppressed by Saddam, responded to his call. But as rebels began to rise up against the defeated dictator, the United States stood on the sidelines. Despite the initial rhetoric of encouragement to rebel against the man that President Bush likened to Hitler, we abandoned them; thousands were slaughtered. We even allowed the Iraqis to use their helicopter gunships to finish the job. Here is how it happened:

At the time of the Gulf War cease-fire talks in Safwan in March 1991, Shiites began a desperate rebellion against Saddam in Basra. General Norman Schwarzkopf met to agree to the cease-fire and surrender terms with the Iraqi representative, General Sultan Hashim Ahmad. The Iraqi general said, "We have a point, one point. You might very well know the situation of the roads and bridges and communications. We would like to agree that helicopter flights are sometimes needed to carry some of the officials, government officials or any member that is needed to be transported from one place to another because the roads and bridges are out." Schwarzkopf was careless in his response, saying there was "absolutely no problem" with this—as long as Iraqi military helicopters did not fly over U.S. positions.

"I want to make sure that's recorded," said the American general, "that military helicopters can fly over Iraq. Not fighters, not bombers." Hashim Ahmad: "So you mean even helicopters that [are] armed in the Iraqi sky can fly, but not the fighters?" "Yeah," said Schwarzkopf. "I will instruct our Air Force not to shoot at any helicopters that are flying over the territory of Iraq where we are not located."   •

And so Schwarzkopf, the victorious American general, unwittingly enabled the terror to begin. Over the next few weeks, Saddam's helicopter gunships were trained against the Shiite rebels of Najaf and Karbala. Saddam murdered at least 60,000 people, whose bodies were flung into mass graves, to be dug up only after his fall in 2003. If Schwarzkopf had denied the Iraqi forces the use of their gunships, Saddam might not have been able to defeat the massive insurgencies.

Even after the slaughter of the rebels had begun, it would have been possible to revoke the license Schwarzkopf had given the gunships. Once again this was not done.

It seems that the administration was above all anxious lest Iraq disintegrate along ethnic or religious lines, leaving Iran the dominant power in the region and thus able to exploit and harness Iraq's Shia majority.

Any hopes that Saddam would be overthrown in a military coup were misplaced. Instead, by exercising his usual brutality and killing tens of thousands of people, Saddam survived. But his demise was still imminently expected in Washington, and so the policy of "containment" was devised. The doleful path of the next twelve years had begun.

Resolution 687—the ceasefire resolution—passed in March 1991, was intended to punish Iraq for its invasion of Kuwait, and to ensure that it never could threaten its neighbors again. It demanded that Iraq unconditionally accept, under international supervision, the destruction, removal, or rendering harmless of all its weapons of mass destruction (chemical, biological, nuclear) and its ballistic missiles with a range over 150 kilometers. It created an inspection system (the UN Special Commission on Iraq [UNSCOM]) to see that these requirements were adhered to. Until this was certified, an oil embargo against the country would remain in place.

UNSCOM had a wider significance than just disarming Iraq. It was part of a thirty-year struggle by the interna-

tional community to create a tapestry of treaties to prevent
the spread of weapons of mass destruction. With it went
the attempt to create a climate of opinion that insisted that
the use of chemical, biological, or nuclear weapons was
wrong. There was no one more ready to defy that convention than Saddam Hussein. "For him," said Richard Butler,
the aggressive Australian diplomat who became executive
director of UNSCOM in 1997, "chemical warfare is as normal as crowd control."

Saddam presumably expected that UNSCOM would be
a typically ineffective UN operation, like the International
Atomic Energy Agency (IAEA), which before the Gulf War
had failed to detect Iraq's extensive nuclear weapons programs. In fact UNSCOM was a uniquely strong organization that was actually empowered to disarm Iraq. Western
and UN officials expected that in order to get the oil flow-
ing again, Saddam would quickly cooperate and surrender
his weapons programs.

He did not. Instead of taking ninety days, as Resolution
687 proposed, the inspectors' task stretched over twelve
years as Iraq constantly denied and defied the inspectors,
lying all the time about the nature and extent of its WMD
programs. The concealment was sophisticated and often
successful. In 1995 UNSCOM came under pressure from
many member states, in particular France and Russia, to give

Iraq a clean bill of health on biological weapons. Their motives were not identical, but each was anxious to promote its commercial links with the Saddam regime, and each wished to be seen as acting independently of Washington.

The inspectors were about to respond to the pressure when suddenly Saddam's son-in-law, Hussein Kamal, defected to Jordan and informed the UN about a massive biological program, documentation of which could be found on a chicken farm. The inspectors discovered that the weapons program was far more extensive than they had previously realized. They learned also that before the Gulf War Iraq had developed VX nerve agent (one of the deadliest chemical weapons) and had weaponized missiles, which they might have launched against the Coalition had it marched on Baghdad.

Despite Iraq's prevarication, obfuscation, harassment of UN personnel, and bald-faced lies, the policy of containment continued.

Charles Duelfer, the deputy executive chairman of UNSCOM, later said that one of the things he had learned in his work in Iraq was the regime's "dedication to all types of weapons of mass destruction." Iraqi officials reiterated that chemical weapons had saved them from the Iranian attacks. Long-range missiles were seen as vital to attacking cities deep in Iran.

The regime had dedicated billions of dollars to the creation of a nuclear weapon as well as chemical and biological weapons. Duelfer observed that Saddam knew "it was a serious blunder to invade Kuwait before they had a nuclear weapon. Regional states know this as well and recognize they will have to accommodate Saddam once a nuclear weapon is achieved."

This was correct. Duelfer's perception was at the core of the long years of Western argument over Saddam's WMD and how to deal with them. Everyone—his Arab neighbors, Israel, Western governments—was terrified that Saddam might acquire nuclear weapons.

But such fears were not often voiced loudly enough. Hypocrisy governed, and another argument was allowed to dominate political debate. Containment was an unsatisfactory policy compromise, and it came under increasing pressure. At the end of 1997 Iraq was cheered by the fact that its friends on the UN Security Council, notably France, China, and Russia, were pressing for sanctions and inspections to be relaxed, if not lifted.

Iraqi propaganda was effective for those who were disposed to believe it; Baghdad convinced much of the world that the UN sanctions were starving a generation of Iraqi children. This was not true: The many exceptions granted for the importation of food and medicine under the UN oil-for-food program meant that no one in Iraq would have starved if Saddam had allowed the distribution of supplies.

But it was convenient to the regime to create starvation and use it as a political weapon. And so it did. Far too many credulous Western journalists swallowed Saddam's propaganda. Arab journalists did the same, and Arab governments, most of which hated Saddam privately, exploited the anti-American feelings generated by such reports.

In 1997 Iraq began to block the weapons inspectors in order to create a crisis. In October the Security Council voted on Resolution 1134, which threatened to impose travel restrictions on Iraqi officials if Iraq continued to do this. The resolution passed the Council, but from Iraq's perspective the important point was that five countries, including three permanent members—France, Russia, and China—abstained. This emboldened Saddam to increase his defiance of the UN inspectors. One issue was his attempt to bar them from vast and lavish "presidential palaces" that he had built for himself while his people starved. At the end of 1997 the United States and Britain threatened a military response.

In early 1998 Kofi Annan, who had become UN Secretary-General a year before, acceded to international pressure from France, Russia, the Pope, and other powerful forces to intercede in an attempt to defuse the crisis. Despite concern in Washington, he flew to Baghdad, met

Saddam, and signed a new agreement with the regime to allow inspections to restart on condition that the inspectors "respect the legitimate concerns of Iraq relating to national security, sovereignty, and dignity."

Inspections did begin again, but Saddam had no intention of respecting either Annan or the international institution he represented. Very soon the Iraqis had reneged on their agreement with the Secretary-General. By December 1998 the position of the inspectors had become untenable. They were withdrawn, and the United States and Great Britain began a short, punitive bombing campaign designed to degrade Saddam's command and control facilities. A few of the targets were WMD sites, but the truth was that the allies simply did not know the concealed location of Iraq's principal WMD programs.

The UN inspectors were not allowed back into Iraq for the next four years—plenty of time for the regime to conceal whatever weapons it had or created during that time.

UNSCOM saw significant successes over the years; the inspectors found many weapons and programs that the regime had tried to conceal. But its experience contained a general lesson for the international community's attempt to stop proliferation. It proved that inspections alone could not deal with the long-term threat posed by a regime determined to defy the world.

The disarmament that UNSCOM accomplished was neither complete nor permanent. Against the full resources of
an entrenched and vicious dictatorship, its powers were
limited. After 1998, when the inspectors were banned from
Iraq, it had no powers at all. UNSCOM's final report in 1999
detailed the weapons that the inspectors still believed were
missing in Iraq. It was a massive, damning indictment.

The inspectors could not account for about 6,000 chemical aerial bombs or for at least seven Iraqi-made missiles
and two Russian-made SCUD missiles. They doubted Iraq's
claim to have destroyed twenty-five missile warheads filled
with bioweapons and could not account for fifty conventional missile warheads.

They reported that Iraq had not accounted for the materials to produce 26,000 liters of anthrax and 1.5 tons of VX
gas. They reminded us that a warhead filled with just 140
liters of VX could kill 1 million people. They wrote that
Iraq's disclosures on biological weapons were "incomplete,
inadequate, and contai[n] substantial deficiencies."

Such threats were by any standard intolerable, but in
early 1999 Western attention had shifted from Iraq to the
Serb persecution of Muslims in Kosovo. Saddam Hussein
and his allies took advantage of the West's Balkan preoccu-
pation. On February 19 a prominent Shiite leader in Najaf
was murdered, almost certainly by government agents. His

death led to the most intense antigovernment riots since the 1991 uprisings. They were crushed by Saddam's security forces, who were reported to be accompanied by troops in white uniforms with gasmasks. The people of Najaf immediately feared that Saddam was about to use poison gas against them. The incident was telling. In order to terrorize his own people, Saddam was prepared to encourage the idea that he might use chemical weapons against them.

Iraq's friends increased the pressure at the United Nations. On April 7, 1999, Richard Butler, the executive chairman of UNSCOM, was barred by the Russians from entering the Security Council chambers, where UNSCOM and Iraq's WMD programs were to be discussed. Butler's diligence had infuriated both Iraq and its advocates abroad. Russia's UN permanent representative, Sergei Lavrov, said they would continue to ban Butler. In Baghdad the government-controlled press exulted.

The administration of President Bill Clinton was well aware of the dangers that Saddam posed. But after vigorous internal debate, the administration had decided to leave Saddam "in his box." Containment would continue.

In the second half of 1999 complicated negotiations took place in the Security Council to craft a new Iraq resolution. Eventually it created a new inspections regime (UNMOVIC) and extended the oil-for-food program. UNMOVIC's terms

of reference continued the weaknesses of UNSCOM, and
Resolution 1284 lifted many of the restrictions on trade with
Iraq. By now this trade was worth some $17 billion, and Sad-
dam's regime was skilled at using its lure to induce France,
Russia, and China to ignore Security Council strictures.

The measure was passed as Resolution 1284 by the Council 11-0 with four abstentions—Russia, China, France, and
Malaysia. The French had promised Washington that they
would support the resolution, but at the last minute Paris
reneged because it learned that Russia was abstaining.
French officials feared that if they did not do the same, Iraq
would switch its lucrative oil-for-food contracts from France
to Russia. Once again the permanent members of the Security Council weakened the UN's own stance against Iraq.

More and more countries began to cooperate with
Baghdad, both legally and illegally. There was no downside.
Trade and smuggling exploded. Iraq used low-cost oil supplies to bribe neighbors like Jordan and Syria. Indeed, Syria
actually opened an oil pipeline between the two countries
and started pumping out some 200,000 barrels of oil per
day in total disregard of UN sanctions. Baghdad started to
insist that foreign companies pay illegal surcharges on
every barrel of oil exported through oil-for-food—to be
paid outside the UN accounting system. Companies and
countries genuflected. It showed that general sanctions can

never succeed over a prolonged period. Too many people profit from breaking them.

Iraqis undoubtedly continued to suffer greatly under the continual assault of terror and economic privation. The sanctions enriched Saddam's ruling class, which deliberately impoverished the common people while blaming the international community. Saddam built more and more sumptuous and extravagant palaces for himself and his sons Uday and Qusay, his partners in the crimes committed against the Iraqi people.

The weakness of Iraqi society enabled Saddam's family to rule even more despotically than ever. The regime gouged out the eyes of children to force confessions from their parents. It fed people into huge shredders, feet first to prolong the agony, or into vats of acid. It forced prisoners to watch their wives, daughters, and sisters being repeatedly raped by guards or having white-hot rods jammed into them.

Uday, Saddam's eldest and most trusted son, was schooled for this task. As a child, he had been taken by his father to watch men being tortured; he was brought up to indulge his tastes in fast cars, drink, and violence against women as well as enemies. Women whom he picked up often disappeared once he had used them; so did those who resisted his will.

In the 1990s Uday was able to control the revenues from

the ministries of oil and foreign trade, and he commanded the band of 25,000 killers known as the Saddam Fedayeen. This made him probably the second most powerful man in Iraq by the mid-1990s. Uday was badly wounded in an assassination attempt in 1996, and after that Saddam handed over more power to his second son, Qusay, who had long been involved in Iraq's ruthless security services, the Mukhbarat.

Qusay was less explicitly violent in his sex life. He did not beat people to death on a whim like Uday. He was more calculating and more cunning—and he committed even more terrible crimes on a far larger scale. From the end of the 1980s, he had been involved in several rounds of prison cleansing—the mass execution of prisoners on the grounds that they were costing the state too much money. And he was in charge of suppressing the Shiite Muslim revolt after the Gulf War in 1991. He was thus responsible for draining the southern marshes, once the home of a quarter-million Marsh Arabs. He and his men made sure that their communities and way of life were completely destroyed. In the late 1990s Qusay's father gave him more and more power; he was made head of the Republican Guards and the Special Republican Guards, the self-styled "elite" troops of the Iraqi army.

Iraq was a wonderland for this gangster family. Max Van

der Stoel, the former UN special rapporteur for human rights in Iraq, had good reason to say that the brutality of the regime was "so grave that it has few parallels in the years that have passed since the Second World War." Since the policy of containment had begun, tens of thousands of Iraqis had been murdered and cast into mass graves.

All this happened as the regime continued to flout UN demands that it disarm.

The policy of containment had other consequences. Above all, it meant that U.S. troops had had to remain in Saudi Arabia since 1991 to deter Saddam from further attacks on the region. Osama bin Laden cited these "armed Christian soldiers" in the sacred land of the two mosques as the ultimate sacrilege that his jihad was to end. It is legitimate to speculate that had Saddam been overthrown in 1991, and had U.S. troops then been withdrawn from Saudi Arabia, Osama bin Laden's greatest proclaimed grievance and rallying cry would have been removed.

Saddam's defiance of the world weakened the United Nations and the international rule of law. Saddam showed contempt for the international system, and he got away with it. He refused to abide by any of the fifteen binding resolutions passed by the Security Council. Nothing could demonstrate better how easy it was for dictatorships to flout international law. His continued pursuit of weapons of mass destruction was documented and apparently unstoppable. His survival provided hope and example to rogue states everywhere.

Furthermore, he had done everything he could to fuel the fire of the Israeli-Palestinian conflict, including paying the families of Palestinian suicide bombers $25,000. Almost all possibilities of progress and development in the Middle East were distorted or corrupted by the continued existence of his regime. Charles Duelfer, the deputy executive chairman of UNSCOM, concluded, "The Security Council's inability to force permanent compliance by Iraq with the very intrusive and stringent disarmament and monitoring measures leads to the case for regime removal."

The crisis of Iraq was pending when President Bill Clinton left office in January 2001. Containment had succeeded in stopping Saddam from attacking any of his neighbors again. But the costs had been immense, and the intelligence suggested that it had not stopped him from pursuing WMD capabilities. The sanctions were being constantly eroded, to the point where they would soon be meaningless. The Iraqi people were suffering greatly. The UN Security Council needed to adopt a new direction; the West had to agree on a new consensus. Into the middle of these challenges strode one of the most controversial and radical U.S. presidents of modern times.

Chapter 2

PRESIDENT BUSH
AND PRIME MINISTER BLAIR

U .S. PRESIDENT George W. Bush polarizes. Richard Nixon did the same through his career, as did Margaret Thatcher. It is a matter of style and substance. The Bush presidency has created almost unprecedented tensions between Europe and the United States.

It is fashionable among European intelligentsia—on the left certainly, but also in more moderate circles—to decry George Bush as the American idiot. Cartoons and articles in European papers constantly try and persuade us that this fool should not be taken seriously. Gerald Kaufman, a Labour member of the British Parliament and a man who sees himself as an intellectual, declared in 2002 that "Bush, himself the most intellectually backward American president of my political lifetime, is surrounded by advisers whose bellicosity is exceeded only by their political, military and diplomatic illiteracy."

George Bush may not be obviously eloquent. He may address his remarks more frequently to Lubbock, Texas, than to Islington or Greenwich Village, but that does not make him stupid. Bush leads a team that wanted to change the world, which perhaps is what makes Europeans so uncomfortable. But perhaps not always anxious to acknowledge this, they take refuge in the claim of stupidity. It is foolish, indeed, for Bush constantly defies the predictions of those who think they are smarter.

In 2000, after he won the Republican primaries, Bush had planned to come to Europe. He did not, apparently in part because of the hostile press his nomination had generated. *Le Monde* referred to "le cretinisation" of U.S. policy. This was perhaps the first introduction of the poison into the bloodstream. Then Bush won the presidency in exceptionally controversial circumstances.

Since then he has become an increasingly ideological president; his policies are often much more radical, both at home and abroad, than expected. He boldly marched in a direction that many people distrusted, cutting taxes, exploiting resources, celebrating personal wealth and free markets.

Many liberal Americans detest his doings. They think he

is destroying the domestic social welfare system and the notion of equity. But in early 2003, before the war in Iraq began, his approval ratings among Republicans were higher even than Reagan's had once been. He had deliberately created the image of a strong decisive leader. Polarization seemed an acceptable price to pay for the demonstration of resolve and vision. Bush's advisers saw his strength as his ability to change the parameters of debate with bold initiatives.

Bush is not a dazzling speaker like Bill Clinton, who could free-associate for an hour on end and convince his audience it has just heard the most important thing since Moses handed down the Ten Commandments. But Bush's aides say that Bush is good at focusing on an issue and carrying it out clearly and easily. As a man who once had a drinking problem, he maintains rigid discipline for himself and sets an example for the White House that is rigorously followed.

Thus W. likes to be seen more as Reagan Junior than as Bush Lite. Mike Deaver, a former senior aide to Reagan, describes him as "the most Reagan-like politician we have seen, certainly in the White House. His father was supposed to be the third term of the Reagan presidency but then he wasn't—this guy is."

Bush, like Reagan, believes that Presidents make their

own mandates. The symbol of Reaganism was his famous phrase "It's morning in America." Bush has as yet coined no such slogan. Perhaps he will not. He lacks Reagan's facility, his eloquence. He also lacks Reagan's extraordinary public charm, though a campaign film of him produced in 2002 did show him displaying a self-deprecating aw-shucks appeal, and he was certainly more charming than his opponent, Al Gore. Clinton had a fabulous, if sometimes superficial, talent to please and to persuade. Bush does not reach out to people with the same ease. He does not seek to persuade. Instead he delivers ukases, a not always likeable habit.

There is another important aspect to Bush—his religion. His critics and enemies, at home and especially abroad, see him as an evangelist with simplistic views, or as a cynic pandering to the zealotry of the religious right, one of the increasingly important forces in American politics.

Bush was brought up Methodist. But religion was not seemingly that important to him during his early years. His Christian rebirth happened when he gave up drinking at the age of forty. He did it through bible study with friends, which led to a powerful religious experience. Now his Christianity is central to his being as well as to his office.

In September 2002 Bush invited religious leaders—three Christian, one Jewish, one Muslim—to meet in the Oval

Office. He talked about the war on terror and asked them to pray along with him. "You know," he said, "I had a drinking problem. Right now I should be in a bar in Texas, not the Oval Office. There is only one reason I am in the Oval Office and not a bar. I found faith. I found God. I am here because of the power of prayer."

Bill Keller of the *New York Times* pointed out, "This kind of born again epiphany is common in much of America—the red-state version of psychotherapy—and it creates the kind of faith that is not beset by doubt because the believer knows that his life got better in the bargain."

Bush's faith is subjective, not scripted or directed. But it is passionate. Not surprisingly he likes to be with people who do not find that weird. He has spoken of bonding with Vladimir Putin, the Russian president (and former head of the godless KGB no less), after Putin told him that his mother had given him a crucifix. He apparently surprised Turkey's new Muslim leader, Recep Tayyip Erdegan, when he told him, "You believe in the Almighty and I believe in the Almighty. That's why we'll be great partners."

He appears to be more at ease with those who believe that the world is more than just the sum of human effort. He is certain he is right.

Bishops in the United States and around the world have denounced the war in Iraq as morally wrong, but Bush has never betrayed doubts about the rightness of the cause. After 9/11 he reminded us that "freedom and fear, justice and cruelty have always been at war, and we know that God is not neutral between them."

Thus it goes deep with Bush. In his 2003 State of the Union address, he spoke of the "power, the wonderworking power" of "the goodness and idealism and faith of the American people." The words "wonderworking power" come from a hymn in which they refer to "the precious blood of the lamb, Jesus Christ."

After 9/11 people came to churches in droves, and many of them then left, having failed to find a comprehensive explanation for what had happened. Bush's religious convictions seem to have provided one: Some analysts argue that he believes in the myth of redemptive violence, which posits a war between good and evil, between God and Satan. For God to win, evil needs to be destroyed by God's faithful followers.

Bush's religious language is alarming to the increasingly secular, agnostic, even atheist Europeans. In America churches are thriving—some 70 percent of the population goes to church. In Europe congregations are diminishing all the time. Europeans are less and less comfortable with God, whereas Bush seems to them alarmingly at ease with Him.

Men like Jacques Chirac of France or Gerhard Schroeder

of Germany almost boast of their rejection of religion. Javier Solana, the European Union (EU) foreign policy chief, said in early 2003 that the role of religion in U.S. policy was becoming a difficulty for Europe. "It is a kind of binary model. It is all or nothing. For us Europeans, it is difficult to deal with because we are secular. We do not see the world in such black and white terms."

But there is at least one important European leader who does share Bush's Christian beliefs: Tony Blair.

When Blair was elected British prime minister in May 1997, he had very little foreign policy experience. Like other prime ministers before, he quickly became convinced of the primacy of Britain's relationship to the United States. At the same time, he was committed to both the ideals and the less-than-ideal structures of the European Union.

In transatlantic terms, Blair was following in a long British tradition, perhaps symbolized most importantly by Roosevelt and Churchill, or Reagan and Thatcher. Not all British prime ministers have been close to their American counterparts; President Nixon did not form keen relationships with either Harold Wilson or Edward Heath, nor did James Callaghan and Jimmy Carter. In some of these cases problems of personality may have intruded.

Blair formed an immediate friendship with Bill Clinton. They and their wives were similar: young, charismatic, left of center (relative to their respective countries), good-looking, and articulate. Both had moved their parties toward the center and talked of a new theory of politics called "the Third Way." On Kosovo and Northern Ireland they worked closely together. Their friendship and political views were so similar that many commentators doubted Blair would ever be able to forge a close relationship with President Bush. They were wrong.

In one important way Blair is more like Bush than Clinton. Though Clinton was also a committed Christian, it would be hard to describe him as a conviction politician. Blair is just that, at least on some major issues. His Christianity informs his life, and it gives him passionately held certainties. Like President Bush—and unlike almost all of his secular European partners—Tony Blair tends to describe major issues in terms of right and wrong, if not of good and evil. He talks of "my covenant to you."

In Britain politicians generally avoid overt declarations of their faith—though Thatcher was an exception. During the buildup to the war in early 2003, Blair was asked by one aggressive BBC interviewer, "Do you and President Bush pray together?" Blair looked shocked by the question. He said they did not.

Blair and Bush are in very different churches and they express their convictions in different ways. But one senior member of the White House to whom I talked said that one of the reasons for the close relationship between Bush and Blair is indeed their shared faith.

There is of course far more to Blair's decisionmaking than his religion. But he brought his views of right and wrong to his conduct of Britain's foreign policy. After he was elected prime minister, Blair was appalled by what he learned of Saddam Hussein's brutality and willful attempts to flout the UN resolutions demanding that he disarm. One senior British politician, Paddy Ashdown, recalled in his diaries that when he went to see Blair on a domestic matter at the end of 1997, all Blair could talk about was the threat from Saddam's WMD. "I have now seen some of the [intelligence] stuff on this," he told Ashdown. "It really is pretty scary. He is very close to some appalling weapons of mass destruction. I don't understand why the French and others don't understand this. We cannot let him get away with it. The world thinks this is gamesmanship. But it's deadly serious."

It was not just Saddam Hussein who aroused Blair's anger. Blair was also horrified by the way in which, after the Dayton Peace Accords of 1995, the focus of Serb violence in the Balkans had shifted to the Serbian province of

Kosovo. The Serbs were actively persecuting the Muslim minority, and a Muslim armed faction, the Kosovo Liberation Army, was growing in strength. Blair played a crucial part in persuading President Clinton that this must be stopped. He was appalled also by the massive abuses of human rights that had been occurring, often almost unchecked, in Africa.

In May 2000 UN Secretary-General Kofi Annan made a direct plea for help from the international community in Sierra Leone. Tony Blair was the only leader to respond. UN forces in Sierra Leone, badly deployed and poorly led, seemed unable to stop an imminent attack on the capital, Freetown, by the same hand-chopping rebels, the Revolutionary United Front, who had sown carnage in the country for more than a decade. Kofi Annan appealed for member states to send a rapid reaction force to Freetown to bolster the UN. Blair agreed when no one else did. Under the cover of evacuating British nationals, he sent some 800 troops to Freetown.

This showed real courage. There was absolutely no political gain to be had in Britain, and yet Blair knowingly took a considerable risk. He was warned by his senior military staff before he dispatched the troops that he could lose up to 100 men. That would have been a disaster in both the human and the political sense. But he sent the mission anyway. In the event a handful of British soldiers were killed during the operation, but the British military presence had the intended effect of deterring the rebel attack. The British then began to build up and train the government's hopeless army. All this was vital in helping save Sierra Leone from continued bloodshed. Blair deserves the credit for that. And he deserves credit for his reaction to 9/11.

The scale of the disaster of 9/11 was at once obvious to almost all Europeans and their leaders. *Le Monde*, the rather grand and traditionally anti-American newspaper of the Paris intellectual class, declared in a headline, "WE ARE ALL AMERICANS NOW." But it was the British who seemed to respond fastest and with the most emotion.

The Queen ordered the Guard at Buckingham Palace to play "The Star Spangled Banner," which reduced many Americans to tears. She sent an exquisite message of sympathy to America in which she concluded, "Grief is the price we pay for love."

Blair was no less swift in understanding the enormity of what had happened. He flew as soon as he could to Washington to promise unconditional support to the Bush administration. He attended President Bush's address to a joint session of Congress on September 20, sitting next to the president's wife, Laura Bush. He was given a standing ovation when the president praised him for his unequivocal support.

Blair deserved the applause. He had understood within minutes of the attacks on the World Trade Center the enormity of what was happening and the wisdom of supporting the United States. Much later, in March 2003, just before military action against Iraq began, he told the House of Commons, "September 11 changed the psychology of America. It should have changed the psychology of the world."

During this crisis, before and after the U.S.-British war in Iraq, Tony Blair played an extraordinary role, especially because he impaled himself on the horns of a dilemma of his own convictions. He not only wanted to offer unconditional support to the United States and to reaffirm the "special relationship" that successive British prime ministers had cultivated. He also wanted to forge agreement with his European partners. Blair cares more than most Britons about the success of the European Union, an increasingly important force that is also increasingly at odds with the United States. Blair tried to have it both ways. The results over the next two years were to be painful for him at home and abroad. His support for President Bush separated him from much of his own party (traditionally suspicious of, if not hostile to, the United States). Sometimes it almost seemed that he had become a hybrid creature: a British neoconservative. But only in foreign affairs.

It is no surprise that the Bush administration was divided on its foreign policy aims and methods, particularly with regard to Iraq, when it came into office. There were those like Secretary of State Colin Powell (and some of Bush Sr.'s advisers, like Brent Scowcroft) who believed that containment, whatever its failures, was wiser than more aggressive alternatives and that Iraq should not be allowed to dominate the U.S. agenda. At the other extreme, there was a group of administration officials (the neoconservatives or "neocons") who believed that until Saddam was removed no progress could be made anywhere in the Middle East or on the issue of proliferation.

In recent months, the neocons have been blamed (less often credited) for almost everything that America has done abroad. They have been held responsible for the war in Iraq, for taking over Washington, for "penetrating the culture at every level." The French magazine *Nouvel Observatuer* calls them the "ideologues of American empire" in an article entitled "After Iraq the World." The BBC broadcast an hour-long television special that began, "This is a story about people who want to run the world their way, the American way [and] scare the hell out of people."

Thereby must hang quite a tale.

The neoconservatives are so called because their intellectual origins were on the left in the late 1960s. They were mocked as neoconservatives by their former friends who stayed on the left. The neoconservatives considered themselves liberals but were disillusioned by the movement away from strong anticommunism after the traumas of the Vietnam War. They were at least as much interested in social policy as in foreign affairs. They included people like Irving Kristol, Daniel Patrick Moynihan, Norman Podhoretz, and Eugene Rostow. Some of them gathered around Senator Henry Jackson in the late 1970s when he campaigned fiercely against Richard Nixon's policy of détente with the Soviet Union.

They drew heavily on the crusading traditions in American thought that characterized Wilsonian ideals, with the important exception that they distrusted international frameworks and collective security. They differed also from conservative realists like Henry Kissinger who espoused balance-of-power politics and managed international relations. Unlike the Kissingerians, they demanded moral clarity in foreign policy. Senator Jackson and his staff went toe to toe with Kissinger in the 1970s over the right of Soviet Jews to emigrate to Israel.

Nowadays, there are few if any Democratic neocons. They are Republicans. But they are far from traditionalists; they were very critical of the views of Republican Trent Lott, for instance, who had to surrender his leadership in the Senate because of racist remarks.

Paul Wolfowitz, now deputy secretary of defense, is one of the neocons' leading intellectual lights. A thoughtful man, he had been an excellent, popular ambassador to Indonesia at the end of the 1980s. He had served at the Pentagon when Dick Cheney was secretary of defense during the first Bush presidency. In 1991, when Cheney was happy to concur with the decision to leave Saddam Hussein in power, Wolfowitz was not. He remained a dedicated proponent of the use of force against Saddam ever after.

In 1992 Wolfowitz and Lewis Libby, who was also in the Pentagon at that time, drafted a defense planning guidance document for Cheney. It was radical. It called for U.S. military preeminence over all of Europe and Asia and proposed that preemptive attacks might be necessary, particularly against states suspected of developing weapons of mass destruction. It called upon the United States to increase military spending to the point where the nation could never be challenged. U.S. military action should be seen as a "constant feature" of the new international landscape. When the document was leaked (perhaps deliberately by its internal critics) to the *New York Times* it caused an uproar. It alarmed more traditional members of the first Bush administration's foreign policy team such as James Baker and Brent Scowcroft. The proposals were watered down before Secretary Cheney published them as an official document, *Defense Strategy for the 1990s.*

During the Clinton era—a dark period for neocons—they were exiled from government and made their views known in several publications like the *Weekly Standard,* edited by William Kristol and owned by Rupert Murdoch, *Commentary,* and the editorial pages of the *Wall Street Journal.* The American Enterprise Institute, a conservative think tank, was the spiritual backbone and home for many, including Richard Perle, an arms control expert from the Reagan era who is popularly known as the "Prince of Darkness," and Lynne Cheney, a conservative cultural critic married to Bush's vice president.

One of the neocons' most important efforts (at least in retrospect) was the Project for a New American Century, founded in 1997 by William Kristol and Robert Kagan. Kagan subsequently wrote the book *Of Paradise and Power,* which made a huge stir in 2003, advancing the thesis that in terms of making foreign policy and war Americans are from Mars and Europeans are from Venus. It was published as the debate over policy toward Iraq hardened and gave a framework to the anger being expressed on both sides of the Atlantic.

The founding statement of the Project for a New American Century called for a "Reaganite policy of military strength and moral clarity" that would promote democracy abroad and "challenge regimes hostile to our interests and values."

The neocons had one overriding objective at that time: the removal of Saddam Hussein. The group wrote to President Clinton that "the only acceptable strategy is one that eliminates the possibility that Iraq will be able to use or threaten to use weapons of mass destruction. In the near term this means a willingness to undertake military action. In the long term it means removing Saddam Hussein and his regime from power."

Several of them are close to the state of Israel, in some cases to the Likud Party. In 1996 three neoconservatives, Richard Perle, Douglas Feith, and John Bolton (all later prominent under President George W. Bush), contributed to an issue paper for the Israeli prime minister, Benjamin Netanyahu. It recommended abandoning the Oslo peace process, insisting on Arab recognition of the Israeli border extending to the River Jordan, and removing the government of Saddam Hussein.

The neocons see the defense of Israel as a crucial test of

America's steadfastness. They believe that Israel will achieve peace not through compromising with enemies but through a grand reordering of its environment, through overwhelming force, and through daring strategic moves. They want to see the entire Middle East transformed by democratization. They consistently argued from the get-go that all this must start with regime change in Iraq.

The charge that many of them are Jewish, and thus biased against Muslims, is undermined by the fact that several were demanding U.S. action to help the beleaguered Muslims of Bosnia in the early 1990s. When the Serbs started to threaten the Bosnian Muslims, President George H. W. Bush had dismissed it as a "hiccup," and Secretary of State Baker said "we have no dog in that fight." Opposition to U.S. inaction was led by people like Paul Wolfowitz, Jeanne Kirkpatrick, and Richard Perle. As Joshua Muravchik, another neoconservative put it, they believed that if Milosevic were able "to get away with aggression, ethnic cleansing and mass murder in Europe [this] would tempt other malign men to do likewise elsewhere." Thus some neoconservatives truly believed that inaction on the part of the United States would make the world a more dangerous place.

There are other common threads in the neocon viewpoint. Neocons tend to believe that we live in a special moment of history, one characterized above all else by

America's unparalleled military power and the opportunity to expand the boundaries of democracy around the world. They argue that this is the time for a grand strategy to assert Pax Americana, that this is the decisive decade in human liberty, and that America must manage a unipolar world.

They are not wedded to stability. Indeed, they are not afraid of challenging the status quo. It is critically important to note that they are wary of permanent alliances. They are attracted to bold geopolitical moves for the expansion of what they see as "American values"—including pluralist political systems and open markets.

They see such values as universal and believe passionately in the special mission to bring American-style democracy to the world. That is particularly true since 9/11. They, like President Bush, tend to see the world in straightforward terms—if not in terms of Manichean absolutes, good and evil.

They want to see, as part of the maintenance of U.S. military preeminence, the development of an antiballistic missile shield, cyber- and electronic warfare capacities, a new generation of nuclear weapons, and weapons in outer space. They argue that the United States should not be constrained from acting unilaterally whenever it sees that its core interests are at stake. Such interests include free access to oil and other vital raw materials, preventing the proliferation of weapons of mass destruction and ballistic missiles, ending global terrorism, and ending the international drug trade.

Until September 11, some of them tended to see the emergence of China as a global power as the greatest threat to U.S. goals. Since September 11, of course, it is the Islamic world that they see as the most important threat to meet. They argue that only the removal of the tyrannical regimes in the Middle East and the creation of democratic states in Islamic societies can deal with Arab underdevelopment and overcome the threat posed by Islamic terrorism.

The ultimate neoconservative aim might well be a global system of free-market democracies, but in the meantime the neocons are content for the United States to ally itself with regional centers of power against smaller, weaker states that are seeking to acquire nuclear weapons and ballistic missiles. Apart from Iraq, such states include North Korea, Iran, Syria, and Libya.

It will come as no great surprise that people who revered Daniel Patrick Moynihan for his attacks upon the "Zionism equals racism" resolution at the United Nations in the mid-1970s have no great regard for the United Nations today. They see it as filled with undemocratic or anti-American nations that seek to use it to constrain the United States.

They have no confidence that evil governments can be reformed. So they must be removed. This means that sovereignty is no longer absolute and to be enjoyed equally by every nation. In other words the neocons dismiss the founding principle of the United Nations. Sovereignty and immunity from attack must, they believe, be relative. The more evil the state, the less sovereignty to which it is entitled. Intervention and the abrogation of sovereignty are legitimate to stop genocide or other crimes against humanity, or in the case of states protecting their own citizens against the threat of terrorism, or in cases where they are acting against clear threats to international security.

These positions are often described as radical, but actually some of the neocon arguments about human rights sound close to mainstream liberal internationalist thought. Indeed, Kofi Annan himself has argued that sovereignty must be qualified and cannot be used any more as carte blanche for mass murder. In summer 1998 he argued that "the UN Charter protects the sovereignty of peoples. It was not meant as a license for governments to trample on human rights and human dignity. Sovereignty implies responsibility, not just power."

He returned to this theme in his address to the UN General Assembly on September 20, 1999, the last of that millennium. Humanitarian intervention in the twenty-first century was his subject, and he pointed out that the notion of state sovereignty—so central to the concept of the United Nations—was being redefined by the forces of globalization and international cooperation. "From Sierra Leone to the Sudan, to Angola to the Balkans to Cambodia and to Afghanistan," he said, "there are a great number of peoples who need more than just words of sympathy from the international community."

There were many other places he could have added, as he acknowledged when he referred to the UN's "willingness to act in some areas of conflict, while limiting ourselves to humanitarian palliatives in many others whose daily toll of death and suffering ought to shame us into action." One such place was Iraq, where the torture of the population over the last thirty years was more terrible than almost anywhere else.

Although the neocons would probably agree with all of that, they go farther. They believe in American exceptionalism. They do not consider the United Nations Charter as the fundamental text governing relations among states. The problem that the UN poses is that it does not and cannot treat the United States as any different from any other member state. The UN cannot, by its very nature, accept that the preeminent global power has rights that are greater than those of every other nation. Most UN officials and member states know that the UN cannot do without the United States, but many of them resent its predominance, and almost all demand that it pay lip service to the equality of nations.

Neocons consider it absurd that the United States should even notionally have parity with, say, dictatorships such as Liberia, North Korea, or Libya. Like many other Americans they also believe that it is absurd to say that U.S. policy should be constrained by the whims of, say, the president of France, wielding his country's Security Council veto over whatever the United States may decide it has to do.

The neocons have more faith in multilateral institutions such as NATO, counting among its membership democratic countries that are, in effect, grouped around the United States. But even NATO has its limitations for neocons, as the case of Iraq graphically showed.

They are skeptical about the whole notion of nation-building, and such skepticism has some basis in reality. The experiences of Cambodia, Somalia, Bosnia, and Kosovo in the 1990s show how hard it is for the international community to graft instant democratic progress onto the landscape and to create civil societies where nothing of the sort had taken root. But the question that must be asked of the neocons is whether they really believe that international neglect of such societies would have been wiser.

It is fair to say that the views of the neocons have played a very important part in U.S. foreign policy making in recent years. But some of the absurd caricatures of their views and their role have tended to inhibit helpful debate.

Thus Michael Lind in the *New Statesman* describes the group as "a product of [an] influential Jewish-American faction of the Trotskyist movement of the 30s and 40s." William Pfaff in the *International Herald Tribune* wrote of their "fanatic" and "totalitarian morality." They are described as having put their ideas over on an ignorant and "easily manipulated" president (Eric Alterman in *The Nation*), his "elderly figurehead" defense secretary (in the definition of Lind), and Colin Powell, "the dutiful servant of power" (Edward Said, *London Review of Books*). The BBC documentary tried to portray the neocons as a sinister cabal. The lead-in announced: "Tonight: Will America's superhawks drag us into more wars against their enemies?"

George W. Bush was not ostensibly a neoconservative when he came to office. He was pragmatic. He talked of a "humble but strong" foreign policy. His principal adviser was Condoleezza Rice, whose first ambition at that time was to improve America's relations with other major powers. He appointed Colin Powell, as cautious a "realist" as could be found, to be secretary of state. However, many of his other appointments gave great power to neoconservatism within the administration, even before September 11.

Both his vice president, Dick Cheney, and his secretary of defense, Donald Rumsfeld, were doughty Cold Warriors who were sympathetic to neoconservative thinking. Each of them recruited from the neocon stable. Cheney chose as his chief of staff Lewis Libby, who had worked closely with the Likud Party and with Paul Wolfowitz at the Pentagon in the early 1990s. Wolfowitz himself became the deputy secretary of defense, Douglas Feith the undersecretary of defense for policy at the Defense Department. Richard Perle became chairman of the Defense Policy Board, a civilian group that advised the Pentagon (he later resigned); Eliott Abrams was made special assistant to the president and eventually senior director for Near East and North African affairs on the National Security Council. John Bolton became undersecretary for arms control and international security at the State Department.

There is little doubt that 9/11 gave neoconservatives the chance to rally the country around their vision of the world and the role that the United States must play in it. Before 9/11 U.S. officials had been prepared to tolerate rogue states and even, in the case of Afghanistan, the presence of bin Laden's army training to attack the United States.

Three days after 9/11, in his speech at the National Cathedral in Washington, President Bush stated that the United States would not hesitate to act alone and would act preemptively to prevent future terrorist threats.

Wolfowitz stated that the United States would "end" states that supported terrorism. He argued in private councils for an immediate attack upon Iraq—his ambition for years. The administration decided to defer this until Osama bin Laden and his Taliban allies were dealt with.

Washington acted in a measured manner after 9/11. Osama bin Laden and Al Qaeda were identified as the perpetrators of the outrage from their camps in Afghanistan. The Taliban regime that had protected them was given time to hand bin Laden over. When it refused, the regime was attacked and driven from power. Western intelligence was alarmed to find evidence of preparations for dirty bombs in the Al Qaeda camps. Osama bin Laden disappeared. He has since resurfaced in videotapes and audio recordings exhorting his followers to continue the jihad against America. Al Qaeda is still very dangerous, but it lacks the secure rear bases and training camps and infrastructure that even a wretchedly poor host country like Afghanistan could offer. Western commitment to Afghanistan since has faltered, but the country is nonetheless better off than it was under the tyranny of the Taliban.

Since 9/11 the United States has developed its doctrines to respond to terrorism. These include prevention, the expansion of military capacity, and preemption. To a greater or lesser degree, they have unsettled America's allies.

Prevention is a familiar concept, extended to justify action preventing all possible attacks on the United States—a broad mandate. Part of prevention is the ongoing expansion of U.S. military capacity and technology, which has a clear deterrence effect. But the radical doctrinal switch was preemption.

There is nothing inherently new about preemption—it has been practiced for centuries. What is new is that members of the Bush administration have stated it so explicitly. The nature of the enemy is also new—terrorists willing to commit suicide in order to kill the maximum number of victims. This cannot be dealt with by conventional methods of containment.

After 9/11 Bush determined that such an attack on America should never happen again. He sees the threat posed by the combination of global terrorism and the proliferation of weapons of mass destruction as completely unacceptable. Put simply, United States must not be constrained in its ability to act militarily and to launch preemptive (including surprise) attacks against states that are thought to threaten U.S. security. As far as the neocons in the administration are concerned, the possible threat posed by terrorism and weapons of mass destruction underlines the need for absolute flexibility.

Thus Bush's description in his 2002 State of the Union

address of three rogue states as the "axis of evil." Bush's speechwriter, David Frum, has explained the process by which his own original phrase, "axis of hatred," became "axis of evil." He argued that the new relationship between terrorist organizations and terror states such as Iraq, Iran, and North Korea resembled the Tokyo-Rome-Berlin axis of the early 1940s. Together they formed an axis of hatred against the United States. The United States could not wait to be attacked by them—it must deal with them first. Given the controversy that the 2002 speech aroused, a controversy that lingers, it is worthwhile quoting in full the relevant passage:

> The Iraqi regime has plotted to develop anthrax and nerve gas and nuclear weapons for over a decade. This is a regime that has already used poison gas to murder thousands of its own citizens—leaving the bodies of mothers huddled over their dead children. This is a regime that agreed to international inspections—then kicked out the inspectors. This is a regime that has something to hide from the civilized world.
>
> States like these, and their terrorist allies, constitute an axis of evil, arming to threaten the peace of the world.

Bush's rhetoric caused a storm of protest and ridicule.

★

The Bush administration's unashamed recognition of the reality of U.S. military and economic preeminence and its commitment to preemption has caused outrage in some parts of the United States and throughout Europe. It is seen as a complete and radical break from all previous views of America's place in the world.

But is it?

By the time the United States entered World War II, if not before, policymakers were convinced that it had supplanted Britain as the world's leader. In 1941 James Forrestal said that "America must be the dominant power of the twentieth century." Henry Luce said it was America's duty not just to win the war against Germany and Japan but also to create an "international moral order" that would spread American principles.

In Newfoundland that year, Roosevelt and Churchill signed the Atlantic Charter, which proclaimed, "Since no future peace can be maintained if land, sea or air armaments continue to be employed by nations which threaten, or may threaten, aggression outside of their frontiers. . . . Pending the establishment of a wider and permanent system of general security . . . the disarmament of such nations is essential." As Lawrence Kaplan and William Kristol point out in their sharp and persuasive book, *The War Over Iraq*, the rationale that Bush and Blair gave for the disarmament of Iraq sounded uncommonly similar.

In 1945 Harry Truman declared that the United States had become "one of the most powerful forces for good on earth" and that the task now was "to keep it so" and "to lead the world to peace and prosperity." In 1947, at the start of the Cold War, Truman declared that "totalitarian regimes imposed on free people, by direct or indirect aggression, undermine the foundations of international peace and hence the security of the United States." And in 1951, explaining U.S. participation in the Korean War, Truman lamented that the allies had not been wiser in the 1930s: "If the free countries had acted together to crush the aggression of the dictators, and if they had acted at the beginning when the aggression was small—there probably would have been no World War II. If history has taught us anything, it is that aggression anywhere in the world is a threat to peace everywhere in the world."

The same words could have been used by Bush with regard to Iraq. Actually they could have been spoken by Clinton as well; the difference is that unlike Bush, Clinton was reluctant to act upon them.

The notion of preemption is not exclusively American, or exclusively in the conservative domain. In 1951 the British philosopher Bertrand Russell, who became one of Britain's most prominent campaigners against nuclear weapons, proposed that the Soviet Union be attacked to preempt it from acquiring nuclear weapons.

In a 1962 legal opinion on the options facing Washington during the Cuban Missile Crisis, the Kennedy Justice Department noted that the UN Charter does not prohibit the taking of unilateral preventive action in self-defense prior to the occurrence of an armed attack.

Now, in the early twenty-first century, threats have changed, and so must the responses to them. The proliferation of weapons of mass destruction, and of terrorists who stalk from the shadows and are susceptible to no kind of deterrence, alter the concept of imminent danger.

After Saddam's overthrow the question lingered as to whether he possessed the great WMD arsenal that justified the administration's war against Iraq. But there was no doubt that Saddam, alone among dictators, had long shown an absolute obsession with obtaining such weapons and had actually used them. He had also refused to accede to more than a decade of international demands that he desist. There was ample reason to believe that he already possessed biological and chemical weapons capacity and that he would seek to restart his nuclear weapons program if he were able. He had the knowledge and the intent—he lacked only the fissile material.

It may have been a mistake for U.S. policymakers to try to establish a link between Al Qaeda and Saddam, a connection to which Tony Blair gave much less emphasis. But whether or not they collaborated directly, the very exis-

tence of a new global terrorist network made Iraq's pre-
sumptive possession of WMD much more threatening.
Theoretically it offered Saddam (and others) a way to
attack the United States by proxy and perhaps without
identification. Prudent policymakers simply could not
ignore the fact that Saddam and Osama bin Laden shared a
hatred of the United States.

Philip Bobbitt, the historian and author of *The Shield of
Achilles*, convincingly made the case that Saddam's regime
had to go:

> Does Saddam, who has twice invaded his neighbours, who
> has the unique distinction of having been the first state to
> annex another member of the UN, who has acknowledged
> seeking nuclear weapons, developing biological weapons and
> using chemical weapons in an unprovoked war of aggression
> against his own citizens, who has violated his ceasefire com-
> mitments, shot repeatedly and continuously at coalition
> forces enforcing the no-fly zone imposed by the UN in 1991,
> really stand in the same position vis-à-vis other countries?

The answer is no. States can and should be judged on
their actions, their intentions, and their capabilities. In the
case of tyrants with a track record like that of Saddam it
would be folly to wait on their increasing their capacities.

Preemptive action against Saddam carried a terrible risk,

but by 2001 containment was being honored more in the breach than the observance. Unless we were prepared to grant Saddam a free hand in the Persian Gulf, Saddam had to be confronted. Had that confrontation been delayed, his record suggested that he might by then have had a vastly increased power to do harm.

The notion of preemption raises fears as well as hackles. But surely everyone would agree that it would have been better if the United States had preempted 9/11 by confronting Al Qaeda and the Taliban before September 2001. There was ample cause. Bin Laden had destroyed two U.S. embassies in Africa, killing hundreds of people (mostly Africans); he had blown up U.S. barracks in Saudi Arabia; he had declared a jihad on the United States; he had bombed the USS *Cole* in Aden Harbor, killing eighteen sailors.

If the United States had acted before September 11 to destroy bin Laden's bases in Afghanistan, 2,700 people who died that day might still be alive. Are not all these deaths a most powerful case for preemption?

Preemption was not inaugurated by the United States in 2003. More than twenty years earlier the same dangerous despot of Iraq inspired Israel's attack against the Osirak nuclear reactor provided by the French. This fast breeder reactor produced more fuel than it consumed. The surplus, Saddam Hussein had publicly boasted, could in theory be used in a nuclear weapon.

Menachem Begin described the reactor as "a technologically advanced version of the final solution." The Israelis chose their moment carefully. They attacked when they did not because the reactor was about to produce a nuclear weapon but because the nuclear fuel was about to be inserted into the reactor; once that was done it would have been impossible to destroy it without spreading radioactive material in a populated area of Iraq.

After long and difficult debate Israel decided to act then because it could not have done so later. Yet Israel was condemned by the world at the time. Why? It should have been clear even then that Israel was assisting not just itself but also the region and the world. Saddam was always said to have regretted that he invaded Kuwait in 1990 without having first acquired a nuclear device. The Israelis had done more than anyone else to set back his lethal ambitions. Israel's preemption was an act of statesmanship carried out with proportionate force.

Preemption carries great risks. In some cases, like that of North Korea, the risks of military action appear to be too great. But there are times when it seems not only necessary but also within the bounds of the possible. Coming from different places, and with very different philosophies, George Bush and Tony Blair came to believe this of Iraq.

In his June 2002 speech to West Point cadets, President

Bush described the dilemma thus:

> The gravest danger to freedom lies at the perilous crossroads of radicalism and technology.... Enemies in the past needed great armies and great industrial capabilities to endanger the American people and our nation. The attacks of September the 11th required a few hundred thousand dollars in the hands of a few evil and deluded men.... If we wait for threats to fully materialize, we will have waited too long.... Our security will require all Americans to be forward-looking and resolute, to be ready for pre-emptive action when necessary to defend our liberty and to defend our lives.

Blair would have agreed with much of that. He and Bush were prepared to take the risks needed to end Saddam's contemptuous defiance of the United Nations and international law, to stop his brutal tyranny over his own people, and to destroy the threat he apparently posed from his continued attempts to acquire WMD.

Many of their allies were not. This dissonance created the greatest split between the Atlantic allies since 1945.

Perhaps it was a disaster waiting to happen.

Chapter 3

THE OLD ALLIANCE

TWICE DURING THE twentieth century Europe proved unable to stand alone against totalitarianism. Without the United States, it might either still be collaborating with Nazism or be under the control of the Soviet Union. It is arguable that the refusal of key European countries to stand up to the threat of Saddam Hussein in 2003 showed that it was still capable of failing the test that it flunked in 1936, when it should have threatened force.

During the Cold War the United States and Europe had a common project: the containment of the Soviet Union. It was a long and exhausting war, but it succeeded, and the Soviet Union eventually collapsed in 1989. That would never have happened but for the consistent deployment of U.S. military and financial power. Europe depended totally on the U.S. security guarantee through World War II and the Cold War—some sixty years.

From the early 1950s onward the United States was in favor of European integration. Why not? Anything that might stop fractious Europeans waging wars that American soldiers had to settle with their own lives was to be welcomed. Moreover, a Western Europe united in common purpose was essential to the struggle against the Soviet Union; a divided Europe could see small nations such as Greece or even Italy lost to the influence of the Warsaw Pact.

The postwar reconciliation of France and Germany seemed impossible when first proposed, a miracle when it was consummated. After the Marshall Plan, the creation of the European Free Trade Area did a great deal to create both prosperity and stability. Closer European cooperation contributed substantially to victory in the vital battles of the Cold War.

There were also major differences in policy during that time. One of the most important followed the Suez debacle of 1956. Anglo-French collusion to seize back the Suez Canal from Gamal Abdul Nasser aroused U.S. ire, and the attempt had to be abandoned. Paris and London reacted in very different ways. The British decided to hew closely to Washington and to build upon what successive British prime ministers liked to call the "special relationship" between the two English-speaking powers. On the whole that has worked to Britain's advantage over the years. But it has prevented Britain from being at the heart of decision-making in Europe.

The French, by contrast, opted no longer to depend entirely on the Atlantic alliance but to create within it (and, it should be stressed, still under the protection of the U.S. nuclear umbrella) a foreign policy more based on perceptions of French self-interest. Charles de Gaulle began to build an independent foreign policy for the European Economic Community. In 1963, having rebuffed Britain's attempt to join that alliance, de Gaulle created a Franco-German treaty of friendship. That, he said, was "the condition and the very foundation of the building of Europe." But to de Gaulle's fury, Konrad Adenauer, the German chancellor, could not persuade the Bundestag to place all German hopes in France. The German parliament insisted on a preamble to the treaty demanding that the government carry out the treaty in such a way as to further the interests of West Germany and its allies, in particular the United States.

As far as de Gaulle was concerned, that made the treaty dead on arrival. But gradually over the coming decades Germany and France did grow closer. At the same time, successive French presidents began to dream that European institutions could be the means of meeting *le defi Americain*—the American challenge. After the fall of the Berlin Wall in 1989, the rules of the game changed instantly. Since 1945 the world had been divided and fought over by two superpowers. Their rivalry dominated everything. With the sudden collapse of the Soviet Union, the United States instantly emerged as the strongest power in the world, no longer constrained by threats from Moscow and benefiting from immense technological advantages.

Sam Huntington, the author of the landmark *Clash of Civilizations*, describes the current world as a "uni-multipolar" system, with the United States preeminent everywhere but having to deal with a series of regional powers such as the European Union, Russia, China, India, Iran, Brazil, and others. "As the only superpower, the U.S. has global interests and actively attempts to promote its interests in every region of the world. This brings it into conflict with the major regional powers, which view the U.S. as the intruder."

America's influence is more than military. U.S. culture, which since World War II has been one of the most powerful forces in the world, has now became almost irresistible as a result of globalization. McDonald's, Nike, Hollywood— they are everywhere. When nineteenth-century Viennese coffeehouses are taken over by Starbucks, the resentment is understandable.

In the 1990s, with globalization apparently unstoppable and Americanization apparently ineluctable, it was perhaps inevitable that a perception gap between Europe and America would grow and contribute to the pent-up demand by many Europeans to express themselves in ways that had not been possible during the Cold War.

Anti-Americanism became the new rock 'n' roll. Or rather, since anti-Americanism is hardly new, and rock 'n' roll was always American, it was an old folksong revived. It made people feel good. Sometimes it is understandable, even justifiable. More often it is a mixture of hypocrisy and delusion.

The awful history of the wars and interventions of the 1990s demonstrates the shallowness. When in 1990 and 1991 the EU and the United States split over how to deal with the fall of Yugoslavia and the consequent conflicts in the Balkans, this seemed to threaten NATO. One EU dignitary declared that the Hour of Europe had come. But it passed—without Europe distinguishing itself. The EU's 1992 Maastricht Treaty was supposed to bring about a new Europe. It created instead a new bureaucracy and new pretensions.

In Rwanda in 1994, when the genocide began, among the first targets of the genocidaires were Belgian soldiers in the UN peacekeeping mission. Ten of them in the capital Kigali were attacked, horribly mutilated, and murdered. There was an understandable outcry in Belgium, and the government evacuated all its troops as quickly as it could. Brussels even demanded that the entire UN mission be withdrawn at the same time. This was not done at once, but the mission was very soon reduced beyond the point of effectiveness.

Up until the beginning of the genocide, the French government—which claimed during the 2002–2003 debates over Iraq to be the moral conscience of the world—was far more supportive of the genocidal extremists in Rwanda than it should have been. The Hutu president, Juvenal Habyarimana, had developed a close relationship with President François Mitterand of France. By the early 1990s hundreds of French paratroopers were fighting with the government to keep the rebel Tutsi at bay. The French saw the Tutsi rebels, coming out of Uganda, as part of an Anglo-Saxon attack on Francophone Africa. Rivalry between *la Francophonie* and *les Anglo-Saxons* was an important subtext to the tragedy.

Some 800,000 people were murdered in Rwanda. It was a collective failure by African nations, by Europe, and by the Clinton administration, whose officials struggled to ensure that the catastrophe in Rwanda was never labeled a genocide, which under international law would have automatically demanded an international response to prevent and punish it.

In the Bosnian conflict all Europe could agree to was to introduce UN peacekeepers, who did indeed save some lives but could not stop the region from falling into chaos. UN Secretary-General Kofi Annan, in his first term of office (1997–2001), did more than any other Secretary-General to promote the organization's moral and strategic responsibilities. He also worked successfully to restore the UN's reputation and support within the United States, particularly in Congress. It was not surprising that he was reelected to a second term by unanimous acclamation in summer 2002.

Annan is the first to admit that there are some tasks that the UN simply cannot fulfill. He is also aware that member states are often all too happy to dump problems on the UN—and that they then fail to provide the necessary resources. This was certainly true in the Balkans.

In Bosnia, the UN peacekeeping deployment reached its nadir in summer 1995 when a handful of ill-prepared Dutch peacekeepers stood aside as the Serbs murdered some 7,000 Muslim men in Srebrenica. The Security Council had demanded that this and other Muslim enclaves in eastern Bosnia be designated UN "safe areas"—but the Council refused to provide either the troops or the mandate that could possibly have made them safe. At that moment of appalling complicity, the United States finally acted, as only it could. The conflicts were ended after the Clinton administration determined to apply force, attacking Serb positions with air strikes until they capitulated, then chaperoning the peace agreement signed in Dayton, Ohio. The European Union proved totally incapable of mustering its own effective response.

Then came Kosovo.

In March 1999 NATO began to bomb Yugoslavia, a member of the United Nations. It did so in order to stop what it saw as unacceptable Serb persecution of the Kosovar Muslims. And it did so without the authority of the UN Security Council. An important precedent was established. The NATO leaders—the United States and Britain—did not seek a Council mandate for attacking Yugoslavia. Why not? Because Russia, Belgrade's principal ally, made clear that it would veto it. NATO went ahead without the backing of the international system.

Moreover, NATO leaders were not keen to advertise it, but they were never able to agree on the legal basis for their action in Kosovo. This does not mean that they did not believe there was a legal basis but rather that their various lawyers used various justifications. Some states relied on the justification of preventing an impending human catastrophe, which they saw as implicit in the UN Charter; others relied on a threat to peace and security within the region; and others put more emphasis on Yoguslav noncompliance with previous UN resolutions. After a long and inconclusive discussion in the North Atlantic Council, the secretary general at the time, Javier Solana, asked if everyone agreed that there was a legal basis. No one dissented, and so they proceeded.

Tony Blair had been the European leader who was most effective in persuading the reluctant President Clinton that, after the shilly-shallying over Bosnia, which had caused so many lives to be lost, action had to be taken swiftly and decisively in Kosovo. After attempts at peace talks with Slobodan Milosevic and other Serb leaders broke down in March 1999, most in Blair's Labour Party were prepared to back war despite the lack of a specific UN mandate. Among them were senior politicians who later refused to endorse the war in Iraq for precisely that reason.

NATO's determination to attack Milosevic without the agreement of the Security Council posed a serious problem for Kofi Annan. He had never ruled out the use of force as a necessary last resort in some international crises. Indeed, in February 1998, as crisis loomed in Iraq over Saddam's refusal to allow UN arms inspectors access to which international law entitled them, Annan called Blair and Clinton "perfect peacemakers" for their willingness to contemplate force to compel Saddam to make concessions. Now Annan had to balance two moral imperatives: the need to protect civilians under assault, and the need to respect the UN Charter.

In a carefully crafted statement, Annan regretted the Yugoslav rejection of a political settlement, then continued, "It is indeed tragic that diplomacy has failed, but there are times when the use of force may be legitimate in the pursuit of peace." He balanced this by pointing out that under the UN Charter the Security Council should be involved in any decision to resort to force.

For his part, Tony Blair declared that Kosovo was the first "progressive" war. He claimed that unlike all previous wars, which were fought on grounds of realpolitik or national self-interest, this one "was fought for a fundamental principle necessary for humanity's progress: that every human being, regardless of race, religion, or birth, has an inalienable right to live free from persecution."

NATO's assault on Yugoslavia and its forces in Kosovo succeeded in driving them out. The United Nations endorsed the subsequent occupation and international administration of the province. As a result of his defeat, Milosevic subsequently fell from power in Belgrade and was later arrested and flown to the Hague to face trial before an international court for crimes against humanity. Kosovo remains an international responsibility and is a province that is still difficult to govern.

But it was quite reasonable for Blair to conclude and declare that the operation showed that the use of force could be legitimate, even without the prior blessing of the Security Council. However, NATO's Kosovo venture exposed serious problems in the alliance. The United States flew the overwhelming majority of the missions, and dropped almost all the precision-guided U.S.-made munitions, and most of the targets were generated by U.S. intelligence. There was just no other way: The Europeans had none of those resources.

The NATO commander, General Wesley Clark, insisted on fighting the war his way, which was intended to be much more decisive than Europe's preferred gradualist approach. It made for a planning nightmare. No one liked the compromises that ensued, and the French were accused of betraying targets to the Serbs.

By the end of the decade, some 200,000 people had died in the Balkans on Europe's watch. It was America that put a stop to it. In 2001, it was only America that could liberate Afghanistan from the Taliban regime. The results in Bosnia, Kosovo, and Afghanistan are far from perfect. But all those countries are better off than they were, and only America could have initiated those changes. American participation is essential to the world.

*

Many Europeans would disagree. As memories of the terrifying Cold War standoff recede, European priorities and relationships have changed. In the unipolar world that followed the collapse of communism, European officials have seemed to feel that they could be more blithe. Germans saw that they no longer needed the United States in the same way. Once united, the two Germanies no longer required a succession of U.S. presidents to repeat the promises of the past. Perhaps even more important, French officials saw the opportunity that Germany's new freedom offered to Paris, which has chafed for years as *les Anglo-Saxons* dominated the world ever more widely. The Franco-German alliance had always been at the heart of European integration, often to the resentment of smaller countries to the north and south.

There is a paradox at the heart of Franco-German leadership in Europe, which has been elegantly (if mischievously) pointed out by the Chilean historian and economist Claudio Veliz. France and Germany may well have "the nicest military uniforms, the shiniest boots, the best martial music parades . . . and the most moving chronicles of battles fought," but they "are also encumbered with the least impressive record in military matters." Germany, he reminds us, last won a war when the Prussians defeated the French at Sedan in 1870; France's last victory he reckons to be at Wagram in 1809. In the twentieth century France had to be "rescued by large numbers of English-speaking soldiers, not once, but twice in a few decades." Then, after 1945, those same English-speakers bailed out the continent, and their troops still remain in large numbers because of European "disinclination or inability, or both,... to provide for their own defence." Trying, indeed, writes Veliz.

The recent struggle over Iraq was made more bitter because at the beginning of the twenty-first century the European Union (at least for some of its members and many of its officials) was diligently attempting to create an alternative to the global power of the United States. EU leaders such as Chris Patten used the word "counterweight" to define the proper relationship between the EU and the world's only superpower. Whether a counterweight can actually be an ally or partner is not clear. Perhaps it is even not meant to be.

The European project, especially in the eyes of the French, started with the simple understanding that no single European power could stand up to the United States in terms of population, wealth, or economic strength, let alone military power. The "pooling" of sovereignty in the interests of creating an "ever closer union" (the words of the 1957 Treaty of Rome) has proceeded apace during the 1990s. The abolition of tariffs, the creation of supranational lawmaking, the surrender of monetary independence and much fiscal policy, the creation of the euro currency—all this and much more create enormous change, one that is anathema to many Americans.

"Imagine if U.S. interest rates were set by a Canadian central banker stationed in Rio" wrote Andrew Sullivan in *The New Republic*. "Imagine if Supreme Court judgements could be appealed to a trans-American court in Brasilia that represented the entire Western hemisphere. Imagine if the dollar was abolished to make way for the 'americano,' a new common currency that included Mexico, Canada, Brazil, Argentina and Chile. Changes on this scale are epic.... It is only natural that they should lead to drastic changes in foreign policy as well."

Enthusiasts for integration now speak of a "United States of Europe." Valery Giscard d'Estaing, the architect of the new European constitution presented in summer 2003, sees it as an entity that "will be respected and listened to as a political power that will speak as an equal with the largest powers on the planet." Romano Prodi, the president of the European Commission, has talked for "a single government" for European countries.

The United States has power and is, not surprisingly, inclined to use it. European states now have very little power. Their inability to act seems to have led to an abhorrence of action. Many European politicians now prefer a system of internationally agreed rules that treat all nations as more or less equal. That is predictable and understandable enough. Europeans have no alternative. They are militarily weak and do not wish to make the sacrifices to be stronger. The numbers tell the story.

In 2003 U.S. defense spending will be $376 billion. Its eighteen NATO partners will spend $140 billion combined. Germany spends 1.1 percent of its gross domestic product on defense; the NATO average in 2.1 percent. The United States spends 3.1 percent, and the gap is widening all the time. Europe can never close it. The Pentagon estimates that only about 3 percent of the world's 2 million men under arms can be "usefully deployed" in the world's new battlefields.

Whatever sacrifices are made, Europe could never—even closely united as the federalists dream—match the power of the United States. And so as Europeans are more and more intent on emphasizing the vital importance of international structures, even those that give equal weight to those who abuse their precepts, America sees less and less merit in treating all countries—large, small, tyrannies, democracies—as of equal significance.

Europe is developing a collectivist outlook that Americans do not share. European countries have spent the last two decades deliberately shedding sovereignty. That is an idea that is completely alien to America, particularly since 9/11.

At the same time, Europe's intellectuals have developed a conventional wisdom, an orthodoxy that has become a dogma. It is at the very least to distrust if not to abhor the United States. With the presidency of George W. Bush, this orthodoxy has become a hysteria. As John Lloyd, the former editor of the *New Statesman*, wrote, European intellectuals "see America as a larger danger than Saddam Hussein and cry out against it. All see it as in terms of empire, domination, greed."

Soon after 9/11, the German actor and playwright Franz Xaver Kroetz said that by planning to attack the Taliban the United States was "guilty of crimes against humanity and is itself a war criminal. To heap suffering on the Afghan Volk is just such a crime. The USA has committed many political crimes over the past several years. I thank God I am not an American." Günter Grass, Germany's most celebrated novelist, attacked America's relations with Iraq over the decades, alleged that oil was the only real interest of Washington, and declared that "the President of the United States embodies the danger that faces us all."

One of the few European intellectuals to defend the United States was Ralf Dahrendorf, the German-born scholar who is also a British peer. He argued that there were three paramount issues in discussing the war in Iraq: First, Western values do exist; second, power is needed to defend them; and third, defense might at times have to be done by force of arms. Roger Scruton was another British intellectual who defended the United States; so did the Canadian author and professor Michael Ignatieff. So have Bernard Kouchner, the former French minister, and some of the French "new philosophers." But most of Europe's intellectuals seem to feel that anti-Americanism is the more comfortable attitude to strike, even when confronted with the undoubted horrors of the Saddam regime. This attitude is seeping into the populace at large.

By early 2002, it was clear that the mass of public opinion in many European countries appeared to be against any kind of intervention to end Saddam's abuse of power, however flagrant his contempt for his own people and for the United Nations itself. And where European peoples ambled, many European leaders were content to follow. Take the strange cases of France and Germany.

Jacques Chirac, president of France, has long been Saddam Hussein's closest foreign friend. Chirac is one of the most controversial French politicians. He was caricatured on French television in 2001 and 2002 by a puppet called

"Super Menteur" or "Superliar." The presidential election campaign of 2002 was dubbed "the crook versus the fascist" because his opponent, Jean-Marie Le Pen, leader of the National Front, was France's most successful extreme right-wing politician.

The French have had many decades to experience the Chirac phenomenon. He has been in politics since the 1970s, and his friendship with Saddam Hussein has flourished since then.

In late 1974, Chirac, the prime minister of France at the time, traveled to Baghdad and met the number-two man in the Iraqi government, Vice President Saddam Hussein. They conducted negotiations on a range of issues, the most important of which was Iraq's purchase of nuclear reactors. In September 1975, Hussein traveled to Paris, where Chirac personally gave him a tour of a French nuclear plant in southern France. During that visit, Chirac said, "Iraq is in the process of beginning a coherent nuclear program and France wants to associate herself with that effort in the field of reactors." Chirac and Saddam then signed an agreement to sell two French reactors to Iraq. One was a 70-megawatt reactor, which came complete with six charges of twenty-six points of uranium enriched to 93 percent—enough weapons-grade uranium to produce three to four nuclear devices. Baghdad also purchased a one-megawatt research

reactor, and France agreed to train 600 Iraqi nuclear techni-
cians and scientists—the core of Iraq's nuclear capability in
the years to come. Even the Kremlin had turned down Saddam's request. Chirac had no such scruples. France also
agreed to sell Iraq $1.5 billion worth of weapons—including
an integrated air defense system (destroyed by the United
States in 1991), about sixty Mirage F1 fighters, surface-to-air
missiles, and advanced electronics.

The Iraqis, for their part, agreed to sell France Iraqi oil
on favorable terms. To celebrate, Saddam gave Chirac a
dinner of fish flown in specially from Baghdad. Chirac
called Saddam "a personal friend and a great statesman,"
and there is little doubt that he meant it. More important,
Saddam told an Iraqi magazine after his return home, "The
agreement with France is the very first concrete step
toward production of the Arab atomic bomb."

It was this overt threat that provoked the Israelis in 1981
to bomb the Osirak reactor. Despite the widespread oblo-
quy to which this led, there is little doubt that Israel did the
world a great service.

The relationship between Saddam and Chirac endured.
In Paris there is constant speculation about its possible hidden aspects. There are still rumors that Saddam helped
finance Chirac's run for mayor of Paris in 1977, after he lost
the French premiership. Another rumor was that Saddam

himself skimmed funds from the Iraqi-French contracts with Chirac's full knowledge. The gossip was such that Iranians referred to Chirac as "Shah-Iraq" and Israelis spoke of the Osirak reactor as "O-Chirac"—before they bombed it.

In 1984 the former French president, Valery Giscard d'Estaing, who was head of state at the time of Chirac's nuclear negotiations with Iraq, claimed that the deal "came out of an agreement that was not negotiated in Paris and therefore did not originate with the president of the republic."

By 1986, when Saddam was deeply embroiled in the terrible war with Iran, Chirac tried to distance himself from the sale of the Osirak reactor. In an interview with an Israeli newspaper, he said, "It wasn't me who negotiated the construction of Osirak with Baghdad. The negotiation was led by my minister of industry in very close collaboration with Giscard d'Estaing." He went on to say, "I never took part in these negotiations. I never discussed the subject with Saddam Hussein. The fact is that I did not find out about the affair until very late." The minister of industry concerned, Michel d'Ornano, denied this account.

There were rumors—which were denied—that the French government had offered to rebuild the reactor after Israel bombed it. In August 1987 the French satirical and muckraking magazine *Le Canard Enchaine* published excerpts of a letter from Chirac to Saddam dated June 24,

1987, and hand-delivered by the French minister of trade, Michel Noir. The letter did not mention reactors—it said that Chirac hoped for an agreement "on the negotiation which you know about," and it spoke of the "cooperation launched more than 12 years ago under our personal joint initiative, in this capital district for the sovereignty, independence and security of your country." In the letter, Chirac once again referred to Hussein as "my dear friend." Chirac and the government confirmed that the letter was genuine and referred to an "essential chapter" in relations between them, but Chirac claimed that any attempt to link the letter to the reconstruction of the nuclear facility was a "ridiculous invention."

Only two possible conclusions can be drawn from this letter: Chirac either was trying, in the midst of the Iran-Iraq War and after his denial of involvement in the first place, to rebuild Iraq's nuclear capability; or he was not. And if he was not, what was he doing that required such oblique language, clearly intended for deniability if revealed? Whatever the answer, it is clear that the relationship between Chirac and Hussein is long and not altogether easy to understand.

After the 1991 Gulf War, Saddam gave an interview to two French writers, Claude Angeli and Stephanie Mesnier, about his relationship with Chirac and other Western politicians. He was clearly not pleased with the fact that governments he had considered close to him had joined the American-led coalition to drive him from Kuwait. The French writers asked Saddam "Has Iraq financially supported French politicians and political parties? In their book *Notre Allie Saddam* [Our Ally, Saddam] Saddam Hussein was quoted as replying:

> Who did not benefit from these business contracts and relationships with Iraq? . . . With respect to the politicians, one need only refer back to the declarations of all the political parties of France, Right and Left. All were happy to brag about their friendship with Iraq and to refer to common interests. From Mr. Chirac to Mr. Chevenement [the socialist former defense minister] . . . politicians and economic leaders were in open competition to spend time with us and flatter us. We have now grasped the reality of the situation [of France's support for the 1991 Gulf War, a betrayal in Saddam's eyes]. If the trickery continues, we will be forced to unmask them, all of them, before the French public.

This threat raised the question of whether Chirac was, all along, being blackmailed by Saddam.

Whatever the truth of that, there were certainly serious

commercial considerations.

In the early 1990s, the French oil company Total/Fina/Elf signed an agreement with Iraq to share oil production in the Majnoon and bin Omar fields as soon as UN sanctions ended. The Majnoon oil field was close to the Iranian border and was estimated to contain 30 billion barrels of oil. Alone it could meet French consumption needs for thirty years. The bin Omar field could produce up to 440,000 barrels per day. The cost of production was reckoned to be only $2 per barrel, making it one of the cheapest in the world, perhaps second only to Saudi Arabia. It would be surprising if any French government did not seek to protect this arrangement with the Saddam regime.

During the late 1990s, under Chirac's watch, France continually sided with Iraq when other members of the Security Council sought to punish Iraq for its flagrant breaches of Council resolutions—which are binding international laws. During this period of sanctions France became one of Iraq's largest trading partners. French exports to Iraq grew apace. "To be blunt," said Ken Pollack, the author of *The Threatening Storm*, "the French have not hesitated to compromise their principles if it meant a greater share of Iraqi trade."

The price for that was continually undermining the UN. Throughout the 1990s France, together with Russia, tried to weaken the UN weapons inspection systems and to give

Iraq the benefit of the doubt. Just as France had reneged on its promise to vote for the resolution establishing UNMOVIC in 1999, so in 2000 Paris bowed to an Iraqi demand that controls on commercial aircraft flying into Baghdad be weakened, despite UN resolutions. The Iraqis showed their gratitude. Even as late as 2001, France sold Iraq $650 million worth of goods, more than any other country. The figure topped $1 billion dollars in 2002.

George Bush's decision to confront Saddam had serious economic implications for France. But there was another, more straightforward explanation for French policy toward Iraq: the power of its Muslim community. This is growing fast throughout Europe, nowhere more than in France. Ten percent of France's population is now ethnically Arab, and it is rising all the time. Some demographers predict that fully a fifth of France will be Islamic in twenty years.

Moreover, fundamentalists are powerful within France's Islamic communities. Mohamed van Guadi, an Islamic expert at Strasbourg University, told Michael Gonzalez of the *Wall Street Journal* that Arab-language radio stations in France carry anti-Semitic and anti-American misinformation. As elsewhere in the Muslim world, preachers rail against America and its intentions.

Alain Madelin, one of France's leading liberal politicians, told the *Journal* that all of this made him very pessimistic.

The French government was doing nothing to counteract the spread of propaganda, and it was therefore becoming ever more its prisoner. "If nothing changes, the French view of the world and the Arab view of the world will become so close, it will be hard to distinguish one from the other."

The *Wall Street Journal*'s Gonzalez also quoted a member of Chirac's inner circle who said that he had warned the president: If he backed the United States over Iraq, he would face nothing short of an "insurrection" from France's 5 million Muslims. And so, the long friendship with Saddam, commercial considerations, the response to the *le defi Americain*, and concern over the reactions of France's Muslims—all these played a part in Chirac's calculations in summer 2002.

And so did his own political survival. In the 2002 presidential election campaign, Chirac was detested. The allegations of personal corruption against him were so serious that he seemed certain to lose. It was convenient for Chirac to deflect attention from his reputation as "Super Menteur" by fighting the election at least in part against the United States and its Iraq policy.

In the second round of the elections, the unhappy French electorate was forced to choose between Chirac and Jean-Marie Le Pen, the leader of France's far-right National Front Party. Faced with the choice of "the crook versus the fascist," 80 percent of those who voted chose the crook.

Jack Straw, the British foreign secretary, recalled later in a television film that the effect was dramatic. "Suddenly you had a right-wing government which was literally off the leash and Chirac, who'd been held back for years, was also off the leash. And he is emboldened and wishes to make it clear that he is in charge and people had better take notice of France in a way they hadn't in the preceding years." Whatever the truth of that, Chirac's electoral success was one closely watched and followed by his friend across the frontier, Gerhard Schroeder.

In summer 2002 Chancellor Gerhard Schroeder of Germany ran for reelection. At first the polls predicted the defeat of his coalition and a victory for the conservative Christian Democrat Party. Schroeder could not run on the economic record of his Red-Green alliance, because it was one of utter failure. He had said at the beginning of his first term that if he failed to reduce unemployment to 3.5 million, he would not deserve a second term. But during that first term, his promise of structural reforms faded. High social spending and heavily regulated labor markets raised the numbers of unemployed to 4 million. By early 2002, the German miracle had become an object of ridicule. "Four million unemployed and it is impossible to buy milk on Sundays," complained veteran opposition politician Otto von Lambsdorff. Thus Schroeder ran against America and in particular against American concerns over Iraq. He accused Washington of "playing around with war."

When one considers the role of the United States in the creation, protection, and encouragement of Germany since 1945, Schroeder's rhetoric appears graceless, reckless, and wrong. The reunification of Germany would never have happened, let alone happened so easily, without full U.S. support. There were pauses on the road to reunification—Margaret Thatcher was not keen—but they were only momentary.

After the fall of the Berlin Wall in 1989, Washington did all it could to help Chancellor Helmut Kohl achieve his ambition to recreate the largest state in Europe. As soon as reunification had been achieved, the allies quietly withdrew from Berlin and the borders they had defended since 1945. As Amity Shlaes of the *Financial Times* put it, "These seemed extraordinary acts of good faith, bankable for at least a generation."

Instead many Germans now appear to resent that for so long after 1945 they had to accept U.S. instructions and that finally they were not able to liberate themselves but needed the might of the U.S. and their other partners to do that for them. Such people liked to overturn reality and argue that Mikhail Gorbachev was far more important to their liberation than was Ronald Reagan; indeed some rationalized that they owed the restoration of their lost freedoms to Soviet and East German restraint, not to U.S. pressure.

After reunification, Germans discovered fully and painfully that the Cold War view of the Communists was entirely accurate. East Germany's economy was risible rather than hugely impressive; quite apart from killing its foes, communism had done its best to kill the environment, and its careless pollution had caused great suffering among its people.

No doubt many Germans acknowledge their liberation and reunification happened only because the military might of the West and its demands for democracy had at last defeated the long-laid, destructive plans of the Kremlin and had brought down the soulless East German regime. But others seem to have decided that discretion was better than valor, that they should improve life at home rather than seek to do for others abroad what had been done by others for them in Germany itself.

Since reunification they have been determined to build up Germany as a leader of the new Europe, that is, the European Union. EU-firstism and anti-Americanism have become the calling cards of the Schroeder party and government. Since 1945 German policy had always been to ally the country to "France in Europe and the United States in the world and for security." Schroeder tore that up.

Through the summer of 2002 Schroeder undermined any attempt to reach an international consensus on Iraq. He talked of Washington's Iraq "adventure." He said that if America attacked Iraq then Germany would remove from Kuwait its small but important detachment of Fuchs armored vehicles that detect biological and chemical weapons. He declared that even if the UN authorized war in Iraq Germany would have no part in it.

The German Chancellor deliberately created an atmosphere of anti-Americanism, and in that context it was not surprising that during the campaign one of his ministers compared George W. Bush to Adolf Hitler. More shocking was the fact that she was not sacked immediately.

All this (and floods in eastern Germany) diverted attention from Germany's economic disasters. America was the evil giant. Saddam was hardly mentioned in the political rhetoric. Even Helmut Kohl's former press secretary, Peter Boenisch, argued fiercely against war in Iraq, declaring that preemption was a "crime" even if it is "made in the USA."

On the eve of the election, a group of prominent French leftists, including Regis Debray and Jacques Lang, declared for Schroeder, who had just appeared at his final rally with the novelist Günter Grass. The anti-American alignment was clear. With the help of the Iraq card, Schroeder narrowly defeated his rivals and barely won reelection on September 22—but at an incalculable cost.

For the first time since 1945 a German election had been fought and won on an anti-American ticket. It was hardly surprising that U.S.-German relations were, as Donald Rumsfeld described it, poisoned. Bush saw Schroeder's behavior as a personal betrayal. He thought, said Bush aides, that in May Schroeder had given his personal assurance that he would not exploit the Iraq issue in his election campaign. Bush has a long memory. He failed to telephone Schroeder to congratulate him.

But from Paris there came bouquets galore. Jacques Chirac was delighted by the victory of the man whom he carefully groomed to help France withstand the overwhelming power of *les Anglo-Saxons* and their plans for removing Saddam.

At the time of Schroeder's reelection the Iraqi dictator was in violation of at least sixteen binding Security Council resolutions that he disarm, and be seen to disarm, stretching back to 1990. It was not just the British and the Americans who believed that he still had weapons of mass destruction.

All the other permanent members of the Council were aware of it on the basis of their own intelligence. Yet every proper effort was still being made to persuade the Iraqis to return to the international fold.

In early July 2002 Kofi Annan traveled to Vienna for talks with the Iraqi foreign minister on allowing UN inspectors back into Iraq. Annan did everything he could to get the Iraqis to agree and warned that U.S. patience was almost exhausted. Still the Iraqis refused to move. To Annan's great disappointment, the talks broke down. Iraq was still utterly intransigent.

By this time the Bush administration, or important parts of it, had decided that the war on terror demanded the end of Saddam Hussein and that in the face of his defiance of international law and the UN only the threat of force could work.

This analysis seemed to be soundly based. Saddam was not the only criminal leader in the world, but he was one who might credibly pose an overwhelming threat to other nations as well as to his own people. Moreover, he was the only one against whom so much international law had been written. It was both immoral and dangerous to allow him to remain in power, posing a vast if unquantifiable threat to the world and, by his defiance, draining the UN of its legitimacy.

But clearly confrontation with Iraq posed huge dangers

and difficulties.

First, Iraq was not a failed state like Afghanistan. It was a ruthless and tenacious dictatorship that terrified, tortured, and murdered its opponents. It had a large army with a supposedly effective elite, the Republican Guards. The determination of the regime to survive could not be underestimated.

Second, the nervousness and hypocrisy of many of America's European allies had its parallel in the Arab world. Most Arab governments loathed and feared Saddam, but few dared to say so. King Abdullah of Jordan, Washington's most likely ally, warned against an attack in July 2002. Arab states would condemn any attack—and so would Arab crowds. There were dire predictions of revolution in the so-called Arab street if the United States intervened.

Third, there was the question of how the United States would do it. By early summer 2002, it was short of weapons expended in Afghanistan; these had to be replenished and in some cases improved. There were not the same bases on offer as in the 1991 Gulf War. There was no equivalent in Iraq of the Northern Alliance in Afghanistan. The risks of Saddam launching a preemptive chemical or biological attack against Kuwait or Israel during a U.S. buildup appeared frightening.

In short, the risks of war were great, but given the nature

of the beast continued inaction was also terrifying. The Afghan precedent showed the dangers of complacency. We had been complacent about Saddam Hussein too long.

There was also a compelling, indeed crucial regional argument for removing Saddam: the impasse of the Israeli-Palestinian conflict. Some European politicians and officials argued that we could not take on Saddam as long as a state of near-war existed in Israel. The opposite could be argued: that as long as Saddam was in power there could be no realistic hope of a solution to Israel and the Palestinians.

In 1991 Israel endured Iraqi attacks with thirty-nine SCUD missiles with exemplary restraint (albeit under very heavy pressure from Washington). Saddam failed to provoke an Israeli counterattack. But a decade later he still wished to destroy Israel. Like other Arab regimes, the Iraqis preached and practiced anti-Semitic hatred. Tariq Aziz, the deputy president who dealt with UNSCOM, told Richard Butler, its executive director, "We made bioweapons in order to deal with the Persians and the Jews." One of Saddam's senior officials said at an Arab summit in 2000, "Jihad alone is capable of liberating Palestine and the rest of the Arab territories occupied by dirty Jews in their distorted Zionist entity." Iraq did everything it could to exacerbate the Palestinian crisis. A crucial by-product of removing Saddam could or should be greater opportunity to move the Israeli-Palestinian peace process forward. But in summer 2002 there was scant European support for the U.S. position.

The Iraqis could not change their own tyrannical government; only outside intervention could do that. There was no better case in the world for such intervention. Tony Blair himself put the issue succinctly later when he told the House of Commons, "When people say to me: 'Why are you risking everything . . . on this issue?' I say I do not want to be the prime minister at whom people point a finger back in history and say: 'He knew perfectly well that these threats were there and he did not do anything about it.'"

Saddam's brutal, aggressive, and illegal behavior since 1991 had been a catastrophe for the Iraqi people and for the region. It had deformed the world. His actions made a mockery of the international legal system as represented by the UN. For more than a decade he had gotten away with it. To continue to connive in his defiance of the UN would weaken it disastrously. By summer 2002 it seemed clear that Washington was right. And Tony Blair was right to support Washington. The tragedy was that other major allies would not agree.

Chapter 4

THE COLLAPSE OF CONSENSUS

O N T H E F I R S T A N N I V E R S A R Y of 9/11, the Iraqi regime did itself no favors by publishing jubilant commemorations of the attacks. *Al Iqtisadi*, a government-controlled Iraqi business newspaper, published a cover story featuring the burning World Trade Center with the headline "GOD'S PUNISHMENT."

Al Ilam, an Iraqi youth newspaper published by the Iraqi Olympic Association, declared that September 11 "shocked the symbols of power in America that some called judgment day. From there they have embarked upon spreading evil with everything they possess."

Aflif-Ba, a magazine controlled by Saddam's son Uday, exulted that 9/11 "exposed that America is incapable of protecting herself and [was] found naked exposed and unable to cover their nakedness.... The simple truth is that it is America that burned itself and now tries to burn the world.... Many view what happened last September as a result of American threats.... This however is not the final chapter."

No, it was not the final chapter.

These rhetorical assaults symbolized Iraq's continued defiance and provocation of the United Nations, building on Saddam's rebuff of Kofi Annan in July. Tony Blair was still determined to make the UN see the scale of the threat posed by Saddam and to enlist its collaboration in facing down the threat. He had the support of Colin Powell, if not of more aggressive members of the U.S. administration such as Dick Cheney.

After fierce argument in Washington, President Bush agreed to Blair's insistence. In an important speech to the General Assembly on September 12, Bush challenged the UN to show that it could be an effective organization and enforce its own binding resolutions made so many times over so many years against Saddam. If it could not, he warned (some saw it as a threat), the UN would be condemned to follow the League of Nations into ignominious failure.

Bush cited the dangers of allowing Saddam to continue his attempts to acquire weapons of mass destruction, and he spoke of the appalling human rights abuses of the regime. (Astonishingly, Amnesty International, which had been diligent at chronicling those abuses, now objected when governments took them up as a reason for facing down Saddam.)

The seven weeks from the opening of the UN General Assembly to November 8, 2002, were dominated by furious public discussion and almost equally furious private arguments among the members of the Security Council. The core issues: the nature of international law, and the wording of any new resolution on Iraq.

Apart from the specifics of Iraq's defiance of the UN over weapons, there was a wider context in which the Iraq crisis had to be considered. The UN's terrible failures in Srebrenica and Rwanda were still on everyone's minds. Long before September 11 Kofi Annan himself had declared that sovereignty could no longer be exploited to protect governments that committed gross abuses of human rights. And other governments could no longer turn a blind eye.

This theme was taken up in an important report, "The Responsibility to Protect," sponsored by the Canadian government and presented to the Security Council in 2001 by the International Commission on Intervention and State Sovereignty. It had a distinguished membership and was cochaired by Gareth Evans, the former Australian foreign minister and now president of the International Crisis Group, and Mohamed Sahnoun, Kofi Annan's special adviser for Africa. Michael Ignatieff, a writer and a professor of human rights, was a member of the commission.

"The Responsibility to Protect" proposed that a state was obliged to protect its people and that if it did not it lost its right to sovereignty.

Evans and Sahnoun made very clear that the UN must enforce this concept of sovereignty. If not, it risked becoming irrelevant. They wrote,

> If the Council fails to act and a military intervention by an ad hoc coalition or individual state follows and respects all the necessary threshold and precautionary criteria—and if that intervention succeeds and is seen by the world to have succeeded—this outcome may have enduringly serious consequences for the stature of the UN itself. This is essentially what happened with the NATO intervention in Kosovo. The UN cannot afford to drop the ball too often on that scale.

*

A dozen lawyers with different opinions can, it goes without saying, dance on the head of a pin.

In 1990, when Iraq ignored the Council's demand to

withdraw from Kuwait, the Council adopted Resolution 678, by which it authorized all member states "to use all necessary means" to enforce its withdrawal "and to restore international peace and security in the area." This was an authorization of military action if Iraq continued its occupation of Kuwait and refused to disarm.

At the end of the consequent war to drive Iraq from Kuwait, the Council adopted Resolution 687, which reinforced all previous resolutions on Iraq, including 678. This crucial resolution remained in force because Saddam's continued defiance and refusal to abide by Iraq's ceasefire obligations meant that the restoration of peace and security in the area had not yet been achieved.

Nor would it be until Iraq had agreed to

unconditionally accept the destruction, removal, rendering harmless under international supervisions, of: all chemical and biological weapons and all stocks of agents and all related subsystems and components and all research, development, support and manufacturing facilities related thereto; and all ballistic missiles with a range greater than one hundred and fifty kilometres, and related major parts and repair and production facilities.

Iraq formally accepted every one of these binding requirements. But over the next eleven years Saddam flouted all of them.

In fall 2002, given this history, it was possible to argue that no new resolution to threaten Iraq with "serious consequences" was required, because Resolution 678 (1990) had never been terminated by the Council. Instead it had been reaffirmed by Resolution 687 (1991). Iraq's threat to international peace and security was ongoing.

Security Council resolutions do not expire, and the requirements of these resolutions were as binding in 2002 as they had been in 1990 and 1991.

Moreover, in 1999, a few months after the inspectors were compelled to withdraw from Iraq, Resolution 1284 replaced UNSCOM with UNMOVIC and required that Iraq allow it unrestricted access. Instead, Iraq had never allowed the inspectors back at all.

There was another important issue—indeed, a vital one in the age of WMD proliferation. That issue was the right of states to take action against Iraq under Article 51 of the United Nations Charter, the right of collective or individual self-defense. It was in the exercise of this right that the UK and United States took military action in Afghanistan in October 2001.

Today, many governments, including those of the United States, Britain, France, other NATO states, and Russia maintain that the right of self-defense applies not only where an armed attack has taken place but also where it is judged to be imminent.

Inevitably, this has to do with the times and the technological possibilities that we have. Judge Rosalyn Higgins wrote, before her elevation to the International Court of Justice, that

> in a nuclear age, common sense cannot require one to interpret an ambiguous provision in a text in a way that requires a state passively to accept its fate before it can defend itself. . . . It is the potentially devastating consequences of prohibiting self defence unless an armed attack has already occurred that leads one to prefer this interpretation—although it has to be said that, as a matter of simple construction of the words alone, another conclusion might be reached.

The right of anticipatory self-defense has been narrowly defined in the past. But the gravity of modern threats requires changes in definition. As the eminent British lawyer Christopher Greenwood wrote in a brief for the Parliamentary Committee on Foreign Affairs in 2002, "the threat posed by a nuclear weapon or a biological or chemical weapon used against a city is so horrific that it is in a different league from the threats posed by cross border raids by men armed only with rifles." This was a reference to the so-called *Caroline* case, a skirmish between the U.S.

and Britain in 1837-1838, which was often taken as a legal precedent. The threat posed by the weapons of 1838 bore no relation to the threat posed by the weapons of the twenty-first century.

Greenwood continued:

The second consideration is the method of delivery of the threat. It is far more difficult to determine the time scale within which a threat of attack by terrorist means, for example, would materialise than it is with threats posed by, for example, regular armoured forces. These would be material considerations in assessing whether Iraq posed an imminent threat to the United Kingdom or its allies. If Iraq did pose such an immediate threat then, in my opinion military action against Iraq for the purpose of dealing with that threat would be lawful.

In London Tony Blair was anxious to abide by the letter of the law. He was assured in fall 2002 that the use of force against Iraq would be justified if the Council passed another resolution justifying action; and if the Council decided that Iraq was in material breach of relevant existing resolutions; and that such a breach constituted a threat to international peace and security in the area. It could also be justified under the right of self-defense if an armed attack by Iraq was reasonably believed to be imminent.

On Thursday, November 7, 2002, the British and the Americans finally presented a new resolution to the Council. It was the result of almost two months of extraordinary and tortuous negotiations, and the compromise wording was hammered out not only by UN ambassadors but also through consultations among Tony Blair and Presidents Bush, Putin, and Chirac—as well as their foreign ministers.

In the discussions over a new Security Council resolution the British frequently referred back to Resolution 678 and its continuing validity. Syria, the only Arab country on the Council at the time, constantly insisted on the need to protect the "dignity" of Iraq. The French and the United States argued over the nature of a "material breach" of any resolution, which Paris insisted only the Council could define. The French were determined not to allow the United States to slip what they called "hidden triggers" into the resolution.

Up until the last moment, French and Russian officials still claimed that they disagreed with the wording. The French said that they were concerned lest the draft resolution make it too easy for the United States to declare that Iraq was in "material breach" and that therefore war was inevitable. They even warned that they were so unhappy with the U.S.-UK draft that they might even veto the resolution—something France had not done to a UN resolution since the Suez Crisis in 1956.

But France faced a Catch-22. They knew that if they split the Security Council they would be encouraging Iraq to defy it—and that would make war more, not less likely, the opposite of their declared aim.

On November 9 Resolution 1441 was passed unanimously by the Council. That was some achievement—and it was the last time the Council would agree on Iraq for many months.

It represented a genuine effort by the United States to use the multilateral process and a success for Blair in keeping Washington committed to the UN, despite all the difficulties, in particular those raised by Chirac. It was also a tribute to the skill of diplomats in New York, especially the British permanent representative, Sir Jeremy Greenstock, and his French counterpart, Jean-David Levitte. The unanimity was an important success for Kofi Annan, who knew that the strength of the UN depended absolutely on its unity. The next few months were to be terrible for Annan as diplomatic warfare broke out and raged around him and the UN came under first verbal and then physical attack.

In Resolution 1441, all fifteen members agreed that Saddam was still in "material breach" of Resolution 678 of 1990 and all subsequent resolutions. Most important, they all agreed that he must once and for all cooperate with inspections, and that he prove that he no longer had WMD. He remained a threat to peace and security in the region. This mattered in the context of later claims that the Americans and the British had exaggerated the scale of Saddam's illegal weapons programs. In Resolution 1441 all members of the Council acknowledged that his conduct still posed an unacceptable danger. It is important to remember that in November 2002 there was widespread conviction that Saddam still had WMD.

The Council resolved that he should be given a "final opportunity" to cooperate fully with the inspectors and disarm; if not, then "serious consequences" would follow. At Anglo-American insistence, the resolution did not say that the Council must meet again to consider any failure by Saddam, but at the insistence of the French it left open the possibility that it could do so. Nor did it specify that yet another resolution was needed before "serious consequences" would be justified. Anglo-American diplomacy seemed to have done very well.

Within a week of the resolution's passage, Iraq was required to say that it accepted it in full. It then had thirty days to provide a full and complete disclosure of all its weapons and weapons programs. Because Iraq had recently announced that it had absolutely nothing to disclose, this new declaration was awaited with interest.

The chief inspector of UNMOVIC was Hans Blix. He was a decent man, but he had not been the first choice of the Americans and British. They had wanted to appoint Rolf Ekeus, the first head of UNSCOM, a diligent Swede whose painstaking investigations in Iraq through the early 1990s had been superlative. For that very reason, Iraq's friends on the Council, in particular France and Russia, had resisted his appointment—in effect on Saddam's behalf. Blix was the compromise choice. Blix had been director general of the International Atomic Energy Agency in the late 1980s—the time when the IAEA had failed to uncover the extent of Iraq's nuclear program.

Now Blix and Mohamed ElBaradei, the current head of the IAEA, were to fly to Baghdad to set in motion the actual inspection process. The task ahead was enormous. Iraq is the size of France. UNMOVIC had about 270 trained inspectors. Each was supposed to have a background in either biological, chemical, or missile technology. Only about a third of them had had some experience of the inspection process that had taken place in the 1990s.

At that time, the UN inspectors had been allowed to interview Iraqi scientists and engineers only with government minders present. Now, as a result of U.S. and British insistence, the new resolution stated that Blix and the IAEA "may at their discretion conduct interviews inside or out-side of Iraq, may facilitate the travel of those interviewed and family members outside of Iraq, and that, at the sole discretion of UNMOVIC and the IAEA, such interviews may occur without the presence of observers from the Iraqi government."

Iraqi officials immediately warned that such an inter-view process would be a violation of their citizens' human rights. And indeed, many Iraqis, terrified of the regime, might actually have preferred to have a government minder present at any interview so that their silence could be proven. Hans Blix warned the Council that "for various pos-sible reasons, some of the persons . . . asked for interviews might decline to speak with us in private or to speak at all."

The subtext to the whole process was simple enough. Would Saddam take this "final opportunity" offered him by the United Nations and cooperate? The point of Resolution 1441, like every previous resolution, was not that the UN had to find proscribed weapons and their production sys-tems but that Iraq had to voluntarily surrender them. If, as Iraqi officials claimed, they had already destroyed all their weapons, then they must prove this. Assertion alone was not enough. The burden of proof was on Iraq, not the inspectors.

Saddam's primary instinct had always been to survive.

With British and U.S. troops beginning to mass on his borders, he might finally understand that the threat to him was now serious and required at least a tactical change. Although Saddam had previously seen WMD as integral to his regime, both as a means of controlling his population and threatening his neighbors, the British hoped that he would now realize that his very future depended on being seen to cooperate fully with the inspectors and to surrender whatever weapons he still concealed.

Without such cooperation the UN's work was futile. Charles Duelfer, the former deputy executive chairman of UNSCOM, had said of UNSCOM's work that "against the full resources of a nation state, with thousands of people and many intelligence and security organs, it was a hopeless endeavour."

In fact Saddam seemed almost from the start to be prepared to breach the obligations he had accepted under Resolution 1441.

In response to the obligation to provide UNMOVIC with a complete description of all Iraq's WMD activities on December 7, Iraqi officials delivered a 12,000-page document to the UN. As soon as it was translated, it became evident that it was an incomplete and untruthful record. Even Hans Blix acknowledged quickly that it contained little that was new. By December 19 the United States and Britain accused Baghdad of already being in "material breach" of the UN resolution.

★

Opposition to Anglo-American tactics had become almost hysterical in many parts of Europe, particularly Germany.

Jeffrey Gedmin, U.S. director of the Aspen Institute in Berlin, said that he had had personal abuse even from German friends. Demonstrators' signs read "BAGHDAD=DRESDEN," "BUSH=HITLER," "NORTH KOREA NEEDS NUCLEAR WEAPONS," and so on. He received letters denouncing him as a war criminal, a coward, a U.S. Goebbels, a Jew "f***er," and he was told to go home. Many Germans (like many French) seemed to wish for a long, drawn-out war so that they could say "I told you so." Only 18 percent of Germans, according to one poll, thought that the United States was a "peace-loving" nation. Four out of five said that Americans could not be trusted.

German intellectuals, like those in other European nations, saw Bush, not Saddam, as the real enemy. They derided him for his manners of speech, his homilies, his Christianity.

It was the same old lyrics—Bush the Christian idiot, Bush the destroyer of Kyoto, Bush the enemy of the United Nations—that the German ruling class was singing. No wonder that hundreds of thousands of Germans demonstrated around the country with posters saying

"F*** You, Bush!"

Did they realize that such conduct would encourage Saddam Hussein? Or did they not care? Did they really not want the United States to help others escape tyranny as it had helped the Germans? At best, this was unreality and naïveté; at worst, it was selfish cynicism.

There seemed to be a feeling that at last Germany could be independent and no longer the junior partner in the Atlantic alliance. Guilt, division, lack of nuclear arms, and no seat on the Security Council had always made Germany's position seem much weaker than France's.

But the assault against Bush may have expressed something deeper, a latent hostility. Jeffrey Gedmin quoted a German editor as saying, "The subconscious has no concept of time. And the truth is, some Germans have never forgotten being humiliated by gum-chewing black Americans who 'liberated' them from Hitler."

A demonstrator's sign in front of the U.S. Embassy in Berlin in early 2003 read, "MR. BUSH, REMEMBER NURNBERG 1945—DEATH BY HANGING!"

France was becoming even more of a concern in Washington. Effrontery might as well have been Jacques Chirac's middle name when in the fall of 2002 he had the temerity to ask Tony Blair how he would justify a war in Iraq to his two-year-old son, Leo.

A preposterous question—it would be much easier for Blair to do this than it would for Chirac to justify to his own grandchildren his own long and shabby relationship with Saddam Hussein. But it reflected the growing bitterness of the fight between Washington, London, and their critics amongst their allies.

On January 21, 2003, after a meeting on counterterrorism at the UN, France's glamorous foreign minister, Dominique de Villepin, ambushed Colin Powell. Without warning, he used the occasion to declare that "today nothing justifies considering military action." Asked if France would use its veto, he replied, "Believe me, that in a matter of principles, France will go all the way to the end." France would do whatever was necessary to prevent war. "We will not associate ourselves with military intervention that is not supported by the international community."

Secretary Powell made little effort to disguise the fact that he was annoyed as much by the discourtesy as by the public declaration of opposition to U.S. policy.

The next day, during the ceremonies celebrating the fortieth anniversary of the Franco-German alliance, Chirac secured the formal support of Germany—which had just become a nonpermanent member at the Security Council—

for France's opposition to the American "hyperpower." From now on the differences between France and Germany and America over Iraq became inescapable.

In Munich, Josckha Fischer discomforted Donald Rumsfeld by announcing in front of the U.S. secretary of defense and the television cameras, "Excuse me, I am not convinced."

Germany's UN ambassador, Gunter Pleuger, called for a concerted campaign against "the U.S. lobby machine." This included trying to dissuade the nonpermanent members of the Security Council—such as Mexico, Chile, Cameroon, and Angola—from voting on a second UN resolution to authorize the use of force in Iraq. It would be better, he wrote, "to force the [United States] to act unilaterally" so that Washington "would be seen as being forced to return . . . with regret to the Security Council when it came to the issue of reconstruction."

The Bush administration grew more and more riled. In revenge for the assaults, Donald Rumsfeld maddened hundreds of French and German officials when he spelled out the problem as he saw it. He divided Europe into "new Europe" (good) and "old Europe" (bad): "Germany has been a problem and France has been a problem," he said. "But you look at vast numbers of other countries in Europe, they're not with France and Germany . . . they're with the [United States]. You're thinking of Europe as Germany and France. I don't. I think that's old Europe."

The fact that this new line in the sand was being drawn by Rumsfeld made it all the more disagreeable to German and French officials (particularly so for the French) because they thought him so uncouth. But there was a good deal of truth in it.

"Old Europe" described parts of Western Europe that had grown rich and comfortable under the shelter of the American umbrella since 1945. In fact old Europe was divided in its allegiances over Iraq. The opposition to America was led by France and Germany, with smaller countries such as Luxembourg and Belgium in close tow, and others behind. In favor of Washington were Great Britain, Spain, and Italy.

The new Europeans were, it is true, more united. They were the nations that had suffered for more than forty years behind the Iron Curtain, where Soviet policy had locked them until the West finally won the Cold War and the Berlin Wall fell in 1989. As the writer Robert Kaplan has pointed out, while West Europeans were demonstrating in the 1960s and 1970s, people in parts of eastern Europe "were getting up at 4 AM to stand in bread lines for their children. For people in this part of Europe, World War II did not end in 1945; it ended in 1989. This part of Europe brings an entirely different perspective."

The new Europeans tended to see the United States as the center that had held during the Cold War. Their political views, if one can generalize, were much starker than those of many in Western Europe. Harsh political choices were not a distant memory, as in the West. They were only now crossing into what they hoped were the sunlit uplands. Their arrival inside or at the doorstep of the European Union was completely changing that organization's political complexion.

The noise made by France, Germany, and their allies on the issue of Iraq was considerable. But Tony Blair was correct to point out that if you counted those countries now preparing to join the EU, the majority was in favor of this difficult venture in Iraq. The ten new countries would have eighty-four votes in the Council of Ministers, as opposed to seventy-four from the antiwar coalition of France, Germany, Belgium, and Luxembourg. If those new members joined forces with the prowar countries of Britain, Italy, and Spain, the combined vote would be emphatic.

This reality threatened French ambitions for the EU to become the counterweight to the U.S. hyperpower. So perhaps it was not so surprising that on February 17 Jacques Chirac himself delivered of one of the classic statements of the war. He chastised the new European countries for their support of the Anglo-American position. They were "infantile" he said. "They have not been very well behaved and rather reckless of the danger of aligning themselves too rapidly with the American position. They missed a great opportunity to keep quiet."

A Czech minister commented that this was just the sort of attitude that East Europeans had suffered through for decades from Brezhnev and other Soviet leaders. They had not expected it from the European Union. Cyril Svoboda, the Czech foreign minister, replied, "We are not joining the EU so we can sit and shut up."

The Latvian president, Vaira Vike-Freiberga, was told by Chirac that NATO was no longer relevant. A Latvian official told the *Financial Times*, "We were shocked by this. We realise now what kind of Europe France wants to make."

No new European country was bolder than Poland. It was continually heading westward, away from the Russian masters who subjected it from 1945 to 1989. It had joined NATO in 1999 and was the biggest of the countries set to join the EU in 2004.

Now Poland infuriated its German neighbor by agreeing to support the Americans. It sent about 200 troops to join the campaign against Saddam. One German newspaper called Poland an American "Trojan donkey." Another said the Poles were "insolent." But the Poles seemed resolute.

Poland's view was straightforward: The United States, its important ally and friend, had decided that Saddam Hussein was a threat to its national security. Poland had no serious objections to this and so accepted Washington's invitation to assist. Poland's own views of the Middle East coincided with those of Washington and London. The government also saw this as an opportunity to help shape a new Europe and a new transatlantic alliance.

In Poland security is a serious business. Poland had suffered generations of humiliation and hardship, caught between the ambitions of Germany and Russia. Germany was now uncertain in its attitudes, Russia still struggling to define its national interest. Poland's neighbor Belarus was run by Europe's last tyrant in an unpredictable manner, and nearby Ukraine was partly democratic but almost wholly corrupt. Security in such a neighborhood is an important matter.

In Warsaw, if not in Paris, it was clear that NATO was the foundation on which the EU was built and Germany reunified. NATO had enabled the EU, an optional extra to Europe. Indeed, NATO was an article of great faith for Poles; they wanted to protect it, not damage it. When France and EU officials presented their fellow Europeans with the option of building Europe into a counterweight to the United States, Polish leaders said no thanks.

Poland was not the only formerly communist East European country that Iraq brought closer to the United States. Hungary, Romania, and Bulgaria all agreed to allow their bases to be used as training or staging posts for the U.S. military. Each was keen to join NATO and to encourage Washington to set up permanent bases on their soil.

Alliances were changing.

In Iraq, the inspections continued with ostensible cooperation but underlying difficulties. Hans Blix and his teams found eleven undeclared empty chemical warheads and 3,000 pages of nuclear documentation. It was reasonable to infer that these were the tips of many icebergs. Washington claimed that most of Iraq's illegal weapons were either deeply buried or distributed in people's home or were being driven around in trucks, always ahead of the inspectors.

On January 27 Blix stunned the Security Council, and delighted the Americans and British, with an outspoken condemnation of Iraqi behavior, saying, "Iraq appears not to have come to a genuine acceptance—not even today—of the disarmament which was demanded of it and which it needs to carry out to win the confidence of the world and to live in peace."

Blix said that Iraq had refused to allow the UN's U-2 spy plane to acquire aerial images; he complained about "disturbing incidents and harassment." He complained that Iraq's 12,000-page dossier of December 7 "does not seem to contain any new evidence" that would resolve the outstanding questions about missing weapons. A litany of these weapons included 6,500 chemical bombs, material sufficient to create 5,000 liters of anthrax, and an unknown quantity of lethal VX in weapon form. Blix also pointed to programs to build possible long-range missiles. He condemned Iraq's early responses to the inspectors and made it quite clear that Saddam was ignoring the demands of Resolution 1441 that he cooperate fully or face "serious consequences."

For his part, Mohamed ElBaradei, in charge of nuclear inspections, presented a generally positive picture of Iraqi cooperation and appealed for a "few more months" to carry on his work "to avoid a war."

This was what a vocal section of the European public wanted to hear. Concern, even anger, at the prospect of war spread across the continent. In Britain Tony Blair became increasingly exposed, with much of his own party, as well as many newspapers and the BBC, standing up against his strong position.

Much of the criticism was abusive. Bishop after bishop lined up to denounce Blair (a committed Christian) as immoral, unchristian, or both. Papers such as the *Mirror* and the *Guardian* attacked him as Bush's poodle, and they abused his alleged owner as an "idiot." The two men's motives were constantly assailed, their convictions dismissed, their intentions misrepresented.

Tony Benn, a veteran left-wing politician and leader of the antiwar movement, declared, "President Bush and Mr. Blair are planning to tear up the charter of the United Nations, to make a war which would be an aggressive war and to kill people, which would be a war crime, and to do it in a way that would endanger world peace over a long period and set the Middle East aflame." Benn arranged to conduct a television interview with Saddam. (It was unctuous and irrelevant.) Before he flew to Baghdad he had the temerity to declare, "I will see women and children who will die in a few weeks because the Prime Minister has decided to kill them."

In the same spirit, the *Daily Mirror* filled an entire front page with a montage of Blair with red-stained hands. It read BLOOD ON HIS HANDS." This was the cover of a two-page rant by journalist John Pilger. He wrote that the Bush administration is "the Third Reich of our times." He denounced Blair as a "liar" and a "coward." There was much more of such stuff from the *Mirror* and from other papers opposed to the war around Europe.

At the end of January 2003 Blair flew to Madrid to consult his most important European ally, Jose Maria Aznar. The Spanish prime minister was, like Blair, defying domestic public opinion to side with the United States. Blair then flew to Washington to persuade Bush that, in light of the opposition at home, he had to be seen to fight for a second UN resolution confirming the case for war made in Resolution 1441.

U.S. officials were not keen on this idea. Many felt that they had already been put through the mill at the UN. They argued that all the necessary authority existed under Resolution 1441 and that any further debate on a new resolution would only arouse further controversy. After all, the French had already made their opposition brutally clear.

But to ease the domestic pressure on Blair, Bush once more acceded. He spoke guardedly of this change of U.S. policy in their joint press conference that day, saying only, "Should the UN decide to pass a second resolution, it would be welcomed if it is yet another signal that we're intent on disarming Saddam Hussein." Under pressure from Blair, he also coupled the Middle East peace process to the fight against Iraq and pledged to make a renewed effort to push for a road map to peace between Israel and the Palestinians.

*

On February 5, 2003, Colin Powell gave a dramatic presenta-
tion to the Council to demonstrate Iraq's pattern of concealment of its illegal weapons. He asserted that for the last
twelve years Saddam had developed very sophisticated techniques to conceal his efforts to produce more weapons of
mass destruction. He played tapes of intercepted conversations between workers at suspicious sites showing that they
had hidden everything before the inspectors arrived. Powell
also revealed the existence of a "higher committee for monitoring the inspections teams" whose sole purpose was to
spy on the inspectors. He presented satellite pictures that
showed how weapons had been moved from suspicious
sites, and the existence of mobile laboratories. He talked
about the pressure placed by Saddam's regime on the scientists and how they were given special training to avoid
telling the truth during interrogations by UN inspectors.

He alleged that Iraq had at least eighteen trucks that
were used as mobile biological agent production vehicles
and that it still "has the wherewithal to develop smallpox."
He claimed that various establishments had dual-use capacities—the ability to produce materiel for weapons and civilian purposes. He asserted that Iraq had purchased

"equipment that can filter and separate micro organisms and toxins involved in biological weapons . . . growth media that can be used to continue producing anthrax and botulinum toxin . . . glass-lined reactors and specialty pumps that can handle corrosive chemical weapons agents." He also alleged that the homes and cars of Iraqi officials were being used to hide documents and computer hard drives, and that rocket launchers and warheads filled with biological agents had been hidden in palm groves.

He showed how Iraq rewarded Palestinian suicide bombers and provided intelligence to terrorist groups in the area. He ended with a statement of Washington's view of the new reality:

> We know that Saddam Hussein is determined to keep his weapons of mass destruction; he's determined to make more. Given Saddam Hussein's history of aggression, given what we know of his grandiose plans, given what we know of his terrorist associations and given his determination to exact revenge on those who oppose him, should we take the risk that he will not some day use these weapons at a time and the place and in the manner of his choosing at a time when the world is in a much weaker position to respond?
>
> The United States will not and cannot run that risk to the American people. Leaving Saddam Hussein in posses-

sion of weapons of mass destruction for a few more
months or years is not an option, not in a post-September
11th world.

In other words, after 9/11 the United States would no
longer accept risks that it had tolerated before.

But Powell did not convince everyone. On February 9
Russia sided with France and Germany in opposing any
attack on Iraq to enforce Resolution 1441. The three coun-
ties proposed instead to triple the number of inspectors in
Iraq and, in some versions of their idea, to persuade Saddam Hussein to turn the country into a virtual UN protec-
torate. This was not a realistic proposal. Saddam would
never have agreed to it. Nor would Washington have given
him the chance.

On February 14 Hans Blix made another report to the
Council. This time, to U.S. dismay, he praised Iraqi cooperation more than he had before, and he criticized some of
the intelligence evidence cited by Colin Powell in his brief-
ing to the Council ten days earlier.

However, there were missing missiles, and missile
engines with longer ranges than allowed, and it was possible that there were more chemical warheads to be found,
so Blix proposed continuing the inspections on an "open-
ended" basis. He repeated that Iraq was cooperating better

on "process" than "substance."

Blix's report was followed by a calibrated, dramatic, if self-serving appeal to the Council by the French foreign minister, Dominique de Villepin: "No one can assert today that the path of war will be shorter than that of inspections. No one can claim either that it might lead to a safer, more just and more stable world. France has said all along: We do not exclude the possibility that force may have to be used one day if the inspectors' reports concluded that it was not possible to continue the inspections."

It was a bald-faced attempt to play to the gallery of the world. De Villepin ended his speech by saying, "In this temple of the UN we are the guardians of an ideal, the guardian of a conscience. This message comes to you today from an old country, France, from a continent like mine, Europe, that has known wars, occupation and barbarity." This dramatic denouement was greeted with an unusual round of applause in the Council chamber, ironic because it was a speech that guaranteed the fracturing of UN consensus.

Around the world millions of people filled their streets for antiwar marches over the weekend of February 15–16. It seemed almost like a resurrection of the Vietnam marches decades ago. Neutralism, pacifism, anti-Americanism, minds closed to the real dilemmas that the proliferation of WMD raised—all were all on display. These were uncanny echoes of the 1960s. The focus of the criticism (or abuse) were the American and British governments and Israel. Palestine banners were carried everywhere. "NO BLOOD FOR OIL!" read one of the most popular (if glib and hypocritical) slogans carried by demonstrators and mouthed at the cameras by those protesting the very notion of any attack upon Saddam. It was difficult, in any of these marches, to see any posters criticizing Saddam Hussein. (On some marches, the organizers specifically banned such sentiments.) People who had protested against the rule of General Augusto Pinochet of Chile were less interested in calling attention to the infinitely worse tyrant of Baghdad.

There were some who understood this hypocrisy. They tended to be men like Vaclav Havel and Adam Michnik, who had suffered under dictatorships themselves. Jose Ramos-Horta, the dissident leader from East Timor, was appalled by the marchers. He wrote, "If the antiwar movement dissuades the U.S. and its allies from going to war with Iraq, it will have contributed to the peace of the dead."

The extraordinary and vital nature of the United Nations was never more obviously on display than during the debate over whether or not a second resolution could succeed. The UN, especially the Council, is the place in which millions of people around the world invest their trust and hopes for a better, more law-abiding world. Sometimes it seems that the world's citizens see the Council as a group of Platonic elders, dispensing justice through wisdom. It is not often that the reality can be said to match this ideal.

The UN was at this time subjected to unprecedented abuse from supporters of the war, who argued the UN was unable to enforce its own resolutions, and their opponents, who claimed that it was useless because the UN could not prevent war.

In fact, as Edward Mortimer, a senior UN official, pointed out, only two wars in the hundreds that have taken place since the UN was created have been fought with Council authorization. They were Korea in 1950 and the Gulf War in 1991. In the case of Kosovo many of those countries that were now so critical of the United States and Britain were happy to proceed without a resolution, and with much less explicit authority from previous resolutions, than those obtained with Iraq.

Some of those who asserted that the UN was now irrelevant seemed not to notice that this very public and rancorous debate was actually taking place there—which alone suggested that the Security Council was still the world's most important forum. And they forgot how much else the

UN did apart from trying (and failing) to reach agreement on Iraq. There were many other resolutions about less contentious places that passed through the Council quietly, if not always unanimously, at this time.

All the time UN agencies like UNICEF and the High Commissioner for Refugees were preparing for humanitarian disaster to follow any war in Iraq. Among the predictions were famine and a massive refugee crisis as hundreds of thousands of Iraqis fled across the borders.

The British, and to a lesser extent the Americans, engaged in a frantic five-week search for the nine Security Council votes needed to pass a second resolution.

The French government apparently urged Washington privately to drop this quest and suggested that if the United States must go forward it could do so on the basis of Resolution 1441 alone. But the left wing of Blair's Labour Party was insisting that without a second resolution an attack on Iraq would be illegal. Blair thought he needed to be seen as going to the wire. The United States demurred on the French suggestion. Bush said, "We don't need a second resolution. It's clear this guy [Saddam Hussein] couldn't even care less about the first resolution. He's in total defiance of 1441. But we're working with our friends and allies to see if we can get a second resolution." And so France, which had previously insisted that a second resolution was essential, began to lobby fiercely to make sure that *les Anglo-Saxons* would never muster the nine votes necessary.

At the beginning of February, the only Council members to support the U.S.-UK position were Bulgaria and Spain. France, Russia, China, Germany, and Syria were absolutely against. There were six undecided votes—soon to be called the "swinging six"—that became the immediate objects of desire on all sides: Pakistan, Cameroon, Angola, Guinea, Chile, and Mexico.

Kofi Annan was in an impossible position. The British and the Americans muttered that he was not being tough enough in enforcing the existing resolutions. Yet the majority of members states demanded that he stand up to "American hegemony"—particularly in light of George Bush.

Annan said that the use of force would not be "in conformity" with the UN Charter unless another resolution was passed. But precedents existed: In the 1990s, West Africa states, including Ghana and Nigeria, intervened in Sierra Leone without a resolution, as Britain had. NATO's campaign in Kosovo had no Council authorization. And Kofi Annan himself had made it clear that coalitions of the willing should be able to act to intervene even if there is no authorization from the Council.

Opponents of war in Iraq predicted appalling consequences for any U.S.-led invasion. There would be massive
resistance by the Iraqi people. There would be a quagmire,
as in Vietnam. Saddam would use his weapons of mass
destruction—though many of the critics claimed he did not
have any such thing. He would attack Israel to force it into
war. The Arab street would erupt in fury throughout the
Middle East. There would be a massive increase in revenge
terrorist attacks.

Eric Alterman in *The Nation* dismissed with contempt
the idea that Iraqis might actually see an invasion as a liberation, declaring that Paul Wolfowitz must be utterly ignorant of history if he believed such a fairytale. Edward Said,
in the *London Review of Books*, denounced not only Wolfowitz but also such experts as Fouad Ajami, Kanan
Makiya, the Iraqi exile author, and Ahmed Chalabi, the
Iraqi opposition leader, for their "rubbish" and "falsifying
of reality" in asserting that a quick war was possible.

To all such critics, the idiotic and antidemocratic George
W. Bush was at the heart of the matter. Said was quoted as
saying in *Al-Ahram*, "In fact, I and others are convinced that
Bush will try to negate the 2004 elections. We're dealing
with a putschist, conspiratorial, paranoid deviation that's
very anti-democratic."

Such analyses and allegations were discussed ad nauseam in corridors, cafés, and councils of the United Nations as the protagonists tried to win over the undecided nonpermanent members. Pakistan seemed likely to abstain. So to muster the necessary nine-vote majority they required all the votes of Mexico, Cameroon, Angola, Guinea, and Chile. These were the nations on whom the "legitimacy" of a war in Iraq apparently now rested. Each naturally had its own agenda.

Mexico's proximity to and increasing economic integration with the United States might seem to lay it open to U.S. pressure, but President Vicente Fox faced strong domestic opposition to war. Backing a new UN resolution could have damaged the prospects of his right-wing National Action Party in midterm congressional elections in July 2003 and weaken his two-year-old presidency.

In Chile, parties from both left and right were pressing President Ricardo Lagos to resist U.S. pressure to back a second resolution. But support for France could have jeopardized a free-trade agreement with the United States that was reached the previous December but had yet to be ratified by both governments.

Cameroon is divided between its Francophone and Anglophone halves. It had joined the British Commonwealth, but Paris was keen that it remain within the Franco-African group that broadly backs France's positions.

However, it had also signed the Africa Growth and Opportunity Act, which in principle obliges signatories to avoid acts "hostile to U.S. national security."

Angola was the African country most likely to side with the United States despite the fact that like other African countries it had supported France's stance at the Franco-African summit. Africa's second largest oil producer, Angola was being courted by Washington as it sought alternative fuel supplies to the Middle East. U.S. oil companies were responsible for driving both exports and inward investments. Potentially one of the richest countries in the world, Angola is one of the most corrupt and therefore among the poorest. It was counting on the United States to exert its influence on international financial institutions to help finance its post–civil war reconstruction.

Guinea was another impoverished dictatorship that had once been a French colony. France was its biggest aid donor, and it was thought to be susceptible to pressure from Paris, though relations had not always been easy. At the same time, Guinea needed extra military aid to combat cross-border incursions from its neighbor, Liberia. It had already enlisted U.S. assistance in military training to strengthen its border defenses. It had also signed a U.S. preferential trade agreement under the Africa Growth and Opportunity Act, which set the same obligation on it as on

Cameroon to avoid acts hostile to U.S. national security.

To ensure that French views prevailed, Dominique de Villepin made a highly publicized tour of the African countries. He was matched by a rather less important and self-important British official, Baroness Amos, a junior foreign office minister who tried to argue the opposite case.

The Africans were also subjected to fierce pressure from their peers. The South African president, Thabo Mbeki, had been urging Africa to unite against intervention in Iraq just as he had been resisting all calls for intervention against the destructive tyranny of Robert Mugabe in Zimbabwe.

Chirac intervened at this moment in Zimbabwe. Britain had been trying to persuade the EU to deny Robert Mugabe access to Europe in protest of his appalling human rights abuses. In a calculated snub, Chirac invited the tyrant to a Franco-African summit in Paris. The British government saw this as another example of grotesque French cynicism.

By the end of the first week in March the six undecideds had apparently decided *against* the Anglo-American resolution. But President Vicente Fox of Mexico was especially anxious not to incur the anger of the United States. He told Jacques Chirac that he would be happy if one of the permanent five members would veto the resolution. That way none of the six would be blamed for the Anglo-American defeat.

Richard Armitage, the U.S. deputy secretary of state, later admitted that the United States had miscalculated. "We thought we could isolate France and just have the others abstain . . . then we would have carried the day. . . . We misjudged the Mexican situation and I think we certainly misjudged France."

The Council is not always right. Remember Milosevic. While Europe hesitated in Bosnia in the 1990s, Milosevic terrorized the region.

In early 2000 he ignored warnings that he would be bombed unless he stopped attacking Kosovar Muslims. A Security Council resolution was impossible because the Russians made clear that they would veto it. Nonetheless, NATO, led by Tony Blair, attacked despite protests from many of those who also would oppose taking action against Iraq. As a result, the Muslims of Kosovo were liberated from ethnic cleansing, and Milosevic eventually fell. Was it immoral to achieve this without a Council resolution? No. The NATO action was given post hoc legitimacy by the Council.

On March 7 Hans Blix and Mohamed ElBaradei gave new, ambiguous reports to the Council. Both said that because of the mounting threat of force Iraqi cooperation had improved since the end of January. But even if Iraq did cooperate fully, completing the inspections would take months.

In response, Colin Powell said, "I was sorry to learn that ... Iraq is still refusing to offer what was called for by 1441: immediate, active and unconditional cooperation.... Despite some of the progress that has been mentioned, I still find what I heard this morning a catalog still of non-cooperation." There was then a lively debate in the Council chamber between the French and British foreign ministers. De Villepin said, "Everyone is faced with the choice of disarming Saddam Hussein peacefully or by force." Jack Straw ignored protocol to reply in the first person: "Dominique, that's a false choice. The choice, Dominique, is not ours as to how this disarmament takes place. The choice is Saddam Hussein's." At the end of Straw's speech, some applauded and de Villepin walked out of the room.

On March 10, Chirac finally dispelled any lingering hope that he might join the United States and Britain at the last moment to ensure that France could help frame the victory in Iraq. Instead he dropped his own bomb. In a television interview he declared that his government would oppose a resolution *quelles que soient les circonstances*—whatever the circumstances.

By announcing that it would veto any Security Council resolution that endorsed Resolution 1441, of which the

French haggled over and eventually approved every single word and of which Saddam was clearly in breach, Chirac deliberately derailed weeks of Anglo-British diplomatic efforts in the Council.

He must have known that this would make war more, not less likely. It was a terrible thing to say, but many British and American politicians said it: Chirac would now have the blood of American and British soldiers on his hands.

Tony Blair had lost his gamble—there would be no second resolution to placate the critics in his party. But he could blame the French by arguing that their veto was unreasonable and that it meant there would never be enough pressure on Saddam to disarm. He said, "This is such a foolish thing to do at this moment in the world's history. The very people who should be strengthening the international institutions are undermining and playing around. Why should Chileans or Africans take the risk of voting for war at the UN if France is going to ensure that their vote is never counted? This is irresponsible."

Over the weekend of March 15–16, Bush, Blair, and Prime Minister Jose Maria Aznar of Spain met in the Azores for a prewar summit. They gave the UN another twenty-four hours to enforce its demands for disarmament or face war within days. The next day they withdrew their resolution from consideration by the Council.

In London the attorney general published a summary of

his legal opinion, which concluded that the war was legal on the basis of Resolution 1441 and previous resolutions. But Blair's critics within his own party were becoming angrier.

There were intellectuals and newspaper editors who loathed America in general and George Bush in particular; there were those who still insisted that it was only about oil and imperialism; there were those who said it must not be done without absolute and clear-cut UN authority; and there were those who claimed it was hypocrisy to intervene in Iraq because there were other regimes that were equally bad.

To these last one could reply "quite so," but there were few other regimes against which there was such a huge body of international law, established by the UN itself. Blair answered this line of attack when he said, "What amazes me is how many people are happy for Saddam to stay. They ask why we don't get rid of Mugabe, why not the Burmese lot? Yes, let's get rid of them all. I don't, because I can't, but when you can, you should."

Blair had failed to secure a new Council vote, but in his struggle, he articulated the case for war more forcefully than any other leader. In September 2002 he had broken with precedent and published intelligence findings on Saddam's weapons. This was a calculated risk, one that would later torment him, as this and a subsequent dossier (which turned out to have been culled in part from the Internet) were subjected to public criticism.

Later, critics ignored the fact that the government's analysis was broadly supported by other states and by such organizations as the International Institute of Strategic Studies (IISS), which published its own conclusion around the same time. The IISS determined that Iraq did not have the ability to create nuclear weapons at the moment but could do so within months if it obtained fissile material from abroad. The IISS also believed that Iraq had retained substantial growth media and biological weapons agents (perhaps thousands of liters of anthrax) and was capable of resuming biological weapons agent production from existing civilian facilities within weeks. On all the key issues, the assessment of the IISS was similar to that of the British, U.S., and many other governments

Intelligence can be wrong, particularly about closed tyrannies where sources are scarce, but it has to be taken seriously when there is nothing else. One senior British intelligence official said to me, "We never know enough." When the U.S. Central Intelligence Agency examined the Al Qaeda camps in Afghanistan, it was alarmed at how far the terrorists appeared to have gone in trying to manufacture a nuclear device.

Back in 2001 Iraqi defectors had convinced German intelligence that Iraq was only two to three years away from
having at least one nuclear weapon. By 2002 the British,
U.S., and Israeli intelligence services believed he would
acquire one or more nuclear weapons by the second half of
the decade unless stopped.

The problem, according to Ken Pollack, a former Clinton national security official and author of *The Threatening
Storm: The Case for Invading Iraq*, was this: Although it was
impossible to know the state of Iraq's nuclear capability,
"we do know that . . . we have consistently underestimated
how far along Iraq has been toward acquiring a nuclear
weapon." Tony Blair also understood that Saddam was
both unpredictable and nurtured the ambition to turn Iraq
into a "superpower" that would dominate the Middle East.

Blair argued that a fundamental choice faced the international community. Either the United States, Britain, and
their allies could continue to be steadfast and compel Saddam to disarm as 1441 and many other binding resolutions
required. Or they could return to the path of least resistance—as proposed by the French, the Germans, and
others—and give the inspectors ever more time. Superfi-
cially, that was the easiest road to take. But it had serious
implications.

The U.S. and British troops around Iraq's borders could

not stay indefinitely in the desert. Their departure would be a huge victory for Saddam, showing that he had outfaced not just the United States but also the United Nations.

The French and the Russians would then argue that containment had worked, that sanctions were no longer needed, and that normal business could resume. Saddam would quietly be able to proceed to develop his WMD ambitions. He would still murder and torture Iraqis. He would eventually have nuclear devices and thus the means to terrorize the entire region. He would seek to dominate the world's oil market. He would threaten Israel. He would be untouchable.

That would not be all. If the prowar alliance backed down, then friends would no longer trust the United States, and enemies would no longer be daunted by it. Radicalization and proliferation would be the new game.

The critics of Blair and Bush seemed to argue that the UN should just forget about the "serious consequences" threatened in Resolution 1441. That would in effect mean saying goodbye to the United Nations as the principle forum for seeking peace and security worldwide. The United States would never take it seriously again.

Months later it emerged that Blair had not told the British Parliament that he had been warned by the government's Joint Intelligence Committee (which collates the views of all intelligence agencies) that there was no evidence that Iraq had provided biological or chemical weapons to Al Qaeda. However, as a parliamentary report later stated, the committee warned that the threat from Al Qaeda would be "heightened by my military action against Iraq" and argued that the collapse of the Saddam regime would "increase the risk of chemical and biological warfare technology or agents finding their way into the hands of terrorists, not necessarily Al-Qaeda."

Blair passed along this warning to some members of his cabinet but not to Parliament. He had taken the view, he said later, that while a war against Iraq might aggravate the war against terror, the greater danger was that in doing nothing a "nexus" between terrorism and weapons of mass destruction could emerge.

On March 18 Blair faced a crucial vote in Parliament. His performance was a tour de force. With passion, he declared that failure to deal with Saddam would lead other nations to think that they too could develop weapons of mass destruction with impunity. "This is a tough choice," Blair told the packed chamber, with a shaking voice. "But it is also a stark one—to stand British troops down and turn back; or to hold firm to the course we have set," he said. "I believe we must hold firm."

He continued: "Our fault has not been impatience. The

truth is our patience should have been exhausted weeks and months and even years ago." The outcome of the Iraq crisis, he added, would "determine the pattern of international politics for the next generation."

The British government's motion to go to war passed 412–149, though 139 Labour members voted for an antiwar amendment.

On March 19, one day earlier than planned, the United States bombed a building in Baghdad in hopes of knocking out Saddam himself (there were intelligence reports that he would be at that location at that time). They missed, and the next day the war formally began.

One week later, the French foreign minister, Dominique de Villepin, made a speech about Iraq in London. He was asked whether France wanted Saddam or the Anglo-American coalition to win the war. He refused to answer. An opinion poll in France showed that a quarter of the French people wanted Saddam to win.

Chapter 5

THE OZYMANDIAS MOMENT

O N APRIL 9, 2003, less than three weeks after the war began, Baghdad fell to the Americans. Saddam and his forces fled.

Victory came far sooner than most commanders or politicians had expected. Suddenly every alliance, prowar and antiwar, had to reconsider preconceptions and revise expectations. Very little that had been predicted about the progress of the war or the nature of a post-Saddam Iraq turned out to be true.

The liberation of Baghdad was symbolized (or at least televised worldwide) as U.S. troops helped pull down a statue of Saddam in central Baghdad. One soldier climbed a ladder and wrapped the Stars and Stripes around the dictator's head. He was instantly ordered to take it off and replace it with an Iraqi flag—to signify that this was liberation, not occupation.

The statue slowly tumbled and, with perfect symbolism, just two rusty pipes were left sticking up from the boots. Jubilant Iraqis trampled upon the dictator's face—the ultimate insult. In the BBC's London studio an Iraqi dissident said through tears, "April 9 is not just spring, it is for Iraqis eternal spring."

It was an Ozymandias moment, one of great optimism for Iraq, for the region, and for the world. Whatever the problems since, one must never forget that April 9 marked the removal of one of the most vile regimes in modern history. It could not have been done any other way.

Kanan Makiya, a prominent Iraqi exile, wrote that the sight of Saddam's bronze head being kicked in the dust "is perhaps the most important image of Iraqi politics of the last fifty years. It was the end of the republic of fear. . . . [April 9] was also a special day for the people of the United States. Their army triumphed. It fought a just war more or less alone and in spite of opposition from countries that put commercial and other interests before the destruction of tyranny."

Almost none of the dire predictions and appalling warnings made by those who opposed the war came to pass. There was no massive resistance. The Iraqis did not fight to the death. Casualties were in fact small given that a whole country had been captured. The United States did not have to destroy Baghdad in order to save it.

Thousands of protective suits and vials of antidotes were found in Iraqi military positions, suggesting that commanders expected chemical or biological weapons to be launched. But no such weapons were used by Iraq. Israel was not drawn into the conflict. The Arab street (if any such thing can be said to exist) did not erupt with fury—indeed, there were fewer demonstrations against the United States across the Middle East than there had been twelve years before during the 1991 Gulf War.

The war did not create a million refugees as pundits had warned—hardly any Iraqis left their country. On the contrary, people who had fled the regime of Saddam Hussein began to return. Nor did the war create a massive famine—indeed the United States had to stop emergency food shipments because they upset the market for farmers. There was no humanitarian disaster. The country did not at once break apart.

Many people at the BBC got it wrong. Eliot Cohen, professor of strategic studies at the Johns Hopkins School of Advanced Studies, pointed out that "supercilious BBC presenters could not contain a sour mirth at the idea of a buffoonish president and his cranky secretary of defence posing as war statesmen. Wrong as well: Their judgments proved sounder than the judgements of those who sneered at them."

The biggest mistake of all, of course, was made by Saddam Hussein. He had apparently calculated that yet again he could rely on friends in the Security Council to wriggle around the UN's latest demands in order to survive and fight another day. He may even have believed that once the inspectors had reported that they had found nothing, sanctions would be lifted and, unimpeded, he could resume whatever weapons programs interested him. Similar calculations had worked before.

All the worst descriptions of Saddam's rule were borne out immediately in the debris of its collapse. People who had lost members of their families to the Baathist terror began to look for graves. By the end of April scores of such horrors had been discovered and partially excavated. Western human rights groups calculated that at least 300,000 people had been murdered by the regime since 1991. Tens of thousands more had been imprisoned and tortured.

Reams of horrifying stories were now told for the first time. At last it became possible to put faces and dates to the many tales of terror told by exiles over the last two decades. Often refugees are accused of exaggerating the horrors they have fled. In some ways the reality of Iraq turned out to be worse than foretold. Within weeks videos and DVDs of police torture, made by the police themselves, were on sale all over Iraq. The horror was there for all to see.

It was hard for Iraqis to believe—indeed, many feared to hope, but that was over now. Arbitrary executions were over and so were official ones—the death penalty was immediately banned. Torture had ended. Speech was freed. Iraq and its population had a future at last. A very difficult future, no doubt. But finally there was hope.

In the TV studios in the West, the armchair retired generals who had insisted that the force was too small to bring down the regime were wrong. However, its strength was its weakness. The brilliantly mobile, relatively small U.S. fighting force was not large enough to keep the peace. The real problems for America in Iraq were just beginning.

Although the invasion was a brilliant tactical success, the first few weeks of the new U.S. administration were a disaster. By mid-May officials in Washington were describing their victory in Iraq as "a catastrophic success." It was abundantly clear that the Pentagon had put far too little thought into the postwar administration of Iraq. It also became clear that everyone had underestimated the rottenness at the heart of Saddam's state. A totalitarian state had become a criminal racket, a putrid edifice that completely collapsed once the gang leaders were chased away. That was not the fault of the United States—it was the consequence of decades of abusive misrule.

One of the earliest crises with which the invading troops was unable to deal was an orgy of looting. It was carried out by many of the scores of thousands of criminals released en masse by Saddam before the war, by Baathists determined to disrupt the victory, and by hundreds of thousands of impoverished and embittered Iraqis suddenly freed from an all-encompassing tyranny.

The looters were ruthless. Government buildings were (for obvious reasons) special targets—seventeen out of Baghdad's twenty-three ministries were destroyed. But hospitals, schools, telephone exchanges, water purification plants, oil industry installations—all were attacked as well. In the agricultural sector fertilizers, pesticides, fuel, and spare parts were stolen. Even flagstones were lifted from sidewalks. Hundreds of tons of copper, aluminum, and steel were soon being sold daily across the Iranian border.

Many of the attacks on pipelines, pumping stations, and the electricity infrastructure were carefully planned and professionally carried out. They had an obvious political motive—to prevent the occupiers from getting the country's economy working again. The U.S. forces were simply not prepared for this, and it was therefore almost impossible to stop it, but sometimes reactions from Washington seemed blasé. "Stuff happens," said Secretary Rumsfeld.

It went on happening. The looting became a systematic attempt by the former Iraqi security forces to make the mechanisms of government inoperable for the United States and, at the same time, to destroy all the records they could. There was no U.S. plan to protect important sites, and so many of them were destroyed. In every sense the looting was a disaster for the Iraqi people and for the occupiers.

As the summer heat intensified, the lack of electricity in homes, of air-conditioning in offices, hospitals, and factories, and of fuel in gas stations caused more and more anger with the occupying forces.

The first attempt to bring order to postwar Iraq was placed in the hands of the Office of Reconstruction and Humanitarian Assistance (ORHA) under retired U.S. General Jay Garner. Under Pentagon orders, some 400 people began to move into Baghdad a week after the war ended; by mid-May the teams had grown to 1,200. Garner was answerable to the U.S. war commander, General Tommy Franks, through the military chain of command. The Pentagon vetted all those appointed to the Garner team, and many competent civilians proposed by the State Department and other agencies were rejected because they were deemed to be inadequately aggressive. The State Department had drawn up a lengthy series of papers in its "Future of Iraq Project." It was ignored. Thus valuable experience in post-conflict situations was lost.

The Pentagon appears to have believed that the United States would walk in, be greeted as liberators, and would be able to take over an intact system from which only the head had been forcibly removed. Within ninety days it would be handing over power to a group of Iraqi tech-nocrats and nonpolitical leaders, whom everyone would welcome and who would cooperate with the world's lead-ing companies to modernize every aspect of Iraq. This was, to be mild, unrealistic.

Garner found that, quite apart from the physical destruction of government buildings, communications between and within departments had also been destroyed by the fall of the regime. "No one knows the whole sys-tem. You know, that's part of totalitarian government. . . . Everything became a manual system," he later told PBS's *Frontline* program.

The frustrations and difficulties of the early weeks were well described by the minister for industry in the new U.S. administration, Tim Carney, one of the few former State Department officials allowed to remain on the team. (He passed muster because Paul Wolfowitz asked him to go to Iraq; he and Wolfowitz had known each other for many

years and had worked together in Indonesia when Wolfowitz was an ambassador.)

I have known and admired Carney's work on the front
line for many years, first in Indochina in the 1970s, where he
was a young State Department officer. Later he served in
the embassy in Indonesia, then went back to Cambodia,
where he worked in a senior position in the UN peacekeeping mission UNTAC in the early 1990s before moving to
the ill-fated UN mission in Somalia. He then became U.S.
ambassador to Sudan and Haiti. All of these were difficult
assignments. But none prepared him for the extraordinary
problems of putting together the pieces of post-Saddam
Iraq.

The Garner team camped in one of Saddam's palaces,
surrounded by U.S. soldiers and isolated from the people. It
was a vast, grotesque building, but few rooms were usable.
The furniture was broken, the windows were smashed,
there was no running water or power. Three former
ambassadors slept together, covered in dust many nights.
There was just one standpipe in the courtyard to wash at.

Carney was shocked to discover the low priority and the
scarce resources given by Washington to the U.S. reconstruction effort. He observed, "Flawed policy and incompetent
administration have marred the follow-up to the brilliant
military campaign to destroy Saddam Hussein's regime."

It was very hard to communicate with the Iraqis. Phones did not work, and U.S. commanders were nervous at letting any civilians out of the compound. They insisted on military convoys, but there weren't enough vehicles.

When Carney finally got to his ministry he found it burned and damaged. "On the ground floor, we were able to salvage a few identity cards and some files on sanctions-busting contracts with Syria and others." Carney's job was both simple and daunting. Before the war, his ministry controlled 96,000 workers in fifty-two state-owned enterprises. They had to get working again.

Reliance on U.S. contractors for everything from power and water to food and phones made things worse. The Pentagon was still using the same military staff structure as during the war. The military commanders had little respect for ORHA and little grasp of its civilian mission. One ORHA official complained in a memo that "ORHA is not treated seriously enough by the command, given what we are supposed to do." Meetings between civilians and military became acrimonious.

Carney felt that no lessons had been learned from recent nation-building efforts in Bosnia or Kosovo. "We in ORHA felt as though we were reinventing the wheel." Garner tried at first to rule through the existing Iraqi government structures, which were controlled by the Baath Party. Washington's initial policy was to keep Baathists on, unless they were known to be involved in gross human rights violations or WMD.

But the invasion had made very clear how deeply the Baathists had reached into Iraqi society, controlling and often terrorizing. About 10 percent of the population—well over 2 million people—were in the party, and almost half a million were in the security services. These were the Saddam loyalists who now bedeviled urban districts and villages throughout the land.

After less than a month, Washington understood that ORHA was not doing well enough. Garner was recalled. ORHA became the Coalition Provisional Authority (CPA). Carney and his colleagues welcomed the arrival of L. Paul Bremer as a presidential envoy on May 12. It seemed to be recognition that the reconstruction effort needed much greater civilian authority.

Bremer, a former top counterterrorism official in the State Department, was acceptable to both State (from whence he sprang) and to the Pentagon, for he had worked closely with Henry Kissinger and had headed a counterterrorism study for the influential conservative think tank the Heritage Foundation. But his views were his own.

When Bremer arrived, security was the biggest problem. As the defeated Baathists regrouped, they began to attack the occupiers, picking off U.S. soldiers singly or in groups. Attacks on civilians were much higher than before the war. In Baghdad fear was widespread.

The U.S. mission reacted too slowly. Many of its problems were self-inflicted. The military communications staff were not brilliant. Raytheon failed to produce a decent communications network; Internet and printer capabilities kept crashing. The cell-phone contractor, MCI, could not create a functioning telephone system for weeks.

Bremer brought in Bernard Kerik, a former chief of the New York Police Department, to create a new Iraqi police force. When he first toured Baghdad, Kerik assumed he was looking at a city ravaged by war, looting, and lawlessness. He then realized that most of the damage had been caused by three decades of rule "by a tyrant who used its natural wealth not to enhance its power plants and sewage and water systems but to aggrandize himself."

Kerik was appalled by what he learned of Saddam's state of fear. Some police stations had torture chambers where they video-recorded assaults upon their victims. "I watched video after video after video of interrogations of Iraqis whose lives ended with the detonation of a grenade that was tied to the neck or stuffed in the shirt pocket of the victim. I watched the living bodies disintegrate at the pull of a pin." He wrote that there is also a tape of Saddam himself "sitting and watching one of his military generals being eaten alive by Dobermans because the general's loyalty was in question."

Bremer radically changed U.S. policy. Perhaps too fast. He disbanded the entire Iraqi army and thereby created enemies of all the men and officers who suddenly had no livelihood and nothing to do except take to the streets and protest the new dispensation. He also reversed Garner's toleration of the Baath apparatus and began a process of de-Baathification. It was not easy. There was an astonishing lack of data, and it was almost impossible for the new American rulers to tell who had joined the Baath party merely to survive and get along, and who had abused their power.

Carney, a veteran of studying Khmer Rouge membership in Cambodia, interviewed scores of Baath party members. They displayed a predictable mix of fear, bravado, and concern. Some Iraqis and some Americans argued that Bremer's purge of the Baathists was "too sweeping." Even junior members at senior management positions needed special exemptions from Bremer to stay on. What to do, for example, with former prisoners of war of Iran? They had automatically been given party membership as compensation upon their eventual return home.

It was hard to get Iraq's paralyzed economy moving again, so Carney and his colleagues decided to throw money at it—literally. They packed wads of money into metal trunks—just under $1 million in $20 bills—and loaded them into the back of Carney's car to distribute as emergency salaries to workers in his ministry.

All decisions were difficult. The only state enterprise still operating was the dairy. Another firm, a producer of chemicals for power generation, water purification, and oil production, needed four megawatts of power to reopen. Colleagues working with the electricity commission had to agree to supply it. But should he restart the textile company? Carney wondered. Could it compete against the Chinese in international markets?

On June 10 Bremer announced an instant $100 million construction fund to speed up the pace of rebuilding and to provide work for Iraqis. Some $45 million was to be spent on urgent building projects, $20 million on refurbishing government ministries damaged by the bombing and by looting, and $35 million on completing public works projects begun before the invasion. "In all of these cases," said Bremer, "work will be done by Iraqi construction companies, creating jobs for Iraqis. We are trying hard to get the economy going by getting money into people's hands."

Carney was desperate to help Iraq. But he wondered whether America would really be able to do it. By the time he left he thought only the determination and imagination of Iraqis themselves could make nation-building a success. "One day, I was standing on a street corner while colleagues were inside looking at a looted grain board facility. I was wearing a class-III bulletproof vest [which will not stop rifle bullets] and my snap-brim, cream-colored, Panama-style fedora. Kids passed by, waving and saying hello. Two girls at that preteen period of sassiness drifted up. The bolder of the two, pulled back by her friend, claimed she loved me and the pair fled in giggles."

"Yes," thought Carney, "but will they love us still in six months? I cannot tell."

Apart from liberating 23 million Iraqis from monstrous tyranny, the overthrow of Saddam and the sudden injection of 150,000 U.S. and British soldiers into Iraq changed the map of the world. The United States announced soon after the capture of Baghdad that it was withdrawing almost all its forces from Saudi Arabia, where they had been stationed to protect the kingdom against Saddam, and moving its regional headquarters to Qatar. The Pentagon also moved to draw down the 80,000 active duty troops in Germany. U.S. strategists argued that they would be more usefully deployed in Bulgaria and Romania, where they would have easier access to the Caucasus and Gulf regions.

Colin Powell visited Syria and warned President Basher Assad that Syria could expect serious consequences if it did not help the United States rebuild a democratic Iraq and if it did not control the activities of terrorist groups such as Hamas, Islamic Jihad, and the Popular Front for the Liberation of Palestine–General Command, which had long had offices in Damascus. (As far as Israel was concerned, Syria did not heed this warning, and on October 5, after a particularly gruesome suicide bombing in Haifa, the Israelis attacked an empty Islamic Jihad training camp in Syria.)

France, Germany, and Russia met for a postwar summit in St. Petersburg on April 12. Their prewar unity had diminished in the face of America's rapid and rather painless military success; they failed to issue a communiqué. The next day the Russian press quoted senior Kremlin officials as saying that relations with America would soon return to normal.

On April 15 Tony Blair flew to Germany to talk to Gerhard Schroeder, and Jacques Chirac called President Bush for the first time in many months. French officials said that Chirac had told Bush he was ready "to act pragmatically and case by case" on Iraqi issues. White House spokesman Ari Fleischer said, "From the President's point of view, he would call it business-like."

Tensions continued. There was still anger in Washington

over France's attempt to deny assistance to Turkey, over Chirac's veto, over France's continuing attempt to stop NATO moving into Afghanistan, and much more. Dominique de Villepin, the French foreign minister and a man who seemed to adore himself rather more than was appropriate, grated in particular. He still insisted that France had always taken the correct position on Iraq, and he even asserted that it was only because Chirac and the Pope had opposed the war in Iraq that the world was able to avoid a Christian-Muslim "clash of civilizations."

On April 29, French, German, Belgian, and Luxembourg leaders met in Brussels. The four refusenik states proposed a new military headquarters for the European Union. This was immediately seen in Washington and London as an attempt to dilute NATO. Colin Powell said that what was needed was more military capacity in Europe, not more headquarters. Previous discussions (known as Berlin Plus) had envisaged any new EU military component using NATO structures. Nick Burns, the U.S. ambassador to NATO, described this new venture as an attempt to drive a stake through NATO's heart.

The U.S. position had consolidated around the idea that it was perfectly acceptable for an ally to *disagree* with U.S. policy (indeed, that was France's democratic right), but downright opposition was a different matter. Washington thought it was not acceptable for an ally actively to campaign against its American friends as de Villepin had continually done.

In Athens, at the first postwar European Union summit, the arguments continued. France and Germany resisted, but Denmark, Spain, Italy, and a number of Central European countries announced that they would send troops to Iraq. Tony Blair declined to pose with other leaders holding olive branches in front of a large white dove of peace.

There were also great differences on the response to terrorism. The French insisted that Washington's forceful reaction was dangerous in that it created more enemies. They claimed that Washington was naive about the hope of building democratic regimes in the Middle East and trampled on the sensitivities of the Arabs. Washington countered that Paris was utterly cynical and happy to deal with the most appalling regimes—such as Saddam's—in the name of some specious stability.

Certainly Europeans were confused. Chirac suggested postwar pragmatism over Iraq, but he also insisted that "we need a means to struggle against American hegemony." Romano Prodi similarly announced that one of the EU's main goals now was to create "a superpower on the European continent that stands equal to the United States."

It was an illusion, to put it mildly. The inequality in

defense spending on each side of the Atlantic alone would make it impossible for Europe ever to become a super-power on a par with the United States. It was more like a spaniel snapping at American heels. Europe was no longer the central theater of geopolitical competition.

Far better if Europe understood that many of the world's problems are common. Terror and proliferation were just two. In a lecture in London, Richard Haass, the director of policy planning at the State Department, said that the EU should make clear to Iran, Syria, and Libya the bad consequences of fomenting terror and making WMD, while the United States has to show them the benefits of desisting. Proliferation was an urgent problem. "We have moved from a world of five nuclear states to one of up to eleven. That should make us all a little nervous." There should be a sustained dialogue on the proper use of force—against governments that kill their own people, that are involved in terrorism and that are making WMD.

Haas pointed to the real need to integrate the Islamic world into the rest of the modern world. Civil society and the rule of law must be urgently promoted.

On Thursday, May 22, the UN Security Council adopted Resolution 1483, which gave legal backing for occupation of

Iraq and ended the thirteen years of sanctions against the state. The only country not to approve the resolution was Syria—whose ambassador chose simply to stay away.

The resolution also allowed oil exports to resume and placed the country under the absolute authority of Washington and London. It lifted restrictions on companies doing business in Iraq. In the future they would be paid from oil revenues, which now passed under U.S.-UK control until a new Iraqi government was formed.

"The liberation of Iraq has cleared the way for today's action," said John Negroponte, the U.S. permanent representative to the UN. Saddam had run a state "unwilling adequately to feed its people, a state in which critical infrastructure projects were left to languish while luxurious palaces were built, and a state in which free political expression was cruelly repressed and punished." He scarcely referred to the weapons of mass destruction, which had formed so large a part of the original rationale for going to war. Few traces of them had yet been found.

France, Russia, and Germany described the UN vote as a compromise. In Paris, Foreign Minister de Villepin said, "In voting for this resolution, France remains true to its principles—the text does not legitimize the war, it opens the way to peace which we must all build together."

The reality was that, however much they might deny it,

France, Germany, Russia, and the other countries that had so vigorously opposed the war in Iraq were now endorsing Anglo-American hegemony in the country. Britain and America would remain in control of Iraq until it set up its own government. Not since the League of Nations gave Britain and France mandates over large parts of the Middle East in the 1920s had foreign countries had such sweeping powers in the region. The resolution did not require renewal and could stay in effect until a new Iraqi government was seated.

The vote authorized the United States and the UK to control Iraq's finances. They would be in charge of the Iraqi Development Fund, based at Iraq's Central Bank, which would disburse all oil revenues. The resolution allowed for the immediate sale of Iraqi oil on the world market.

Iraq has the second largest reserves of oil in the world, but levels of output had fallen to between 300,000 and 600,000 barrels a day. Investment of around $1.7 billion was probably needed to restore production capacity to the 3.5 million barrels a day that Iraq enjoyed before the invasion of Kuwait in 1990. Another $3 billion would be needed to bring on stream new oil fields discovered in the 1970s but not yet exploited.

Immediately, Iraq was not even able to meet domestic

needs, and long lines of cars stretched around gas stations throughout the country. War damage had been much less than in 1991, and its three biggest refineries were back in production. But looting was inflicting serious damage on this sector as on all others.

Iraq's reconstruction was often reckoned to be likely to cost at least $100 billion, the largest such project since the United States helped rebuild Europe through the Marshall Plan. Obviously all the world's companies wanted to be there. At first, the only two contracts awarded were emergency deals for two American giants, Halliburton and Bechtel, to extinguish oil-well fires and repair Iraq's infrastructure. These two contracts had aroused adverse comment because both companies were close to the U.S. administration—indeed Vice President Dick Cheney had been chief executive of Halliburton until he ran for office. And the contracts were awarded without competitive bidding. This was neither proper nor wise.

Resolution 1483 also appointed a UN special representative to have independent responsibilities over a wide range of humanitarian and reconstruction activities and to work with the occupying powers and the people of Iraq to form a government. This was a difficult role for the UN, since so many members were opposed to the occupation. Its role in Baghdad would be rather ambiguous, supporting the independence of the Iraqi people and working with the occupiers while not appearing to endorse the invasion.

Secretary-General Kofi Annan was urged by many governments, including Britain and America, to put in charge of the mission Sergio Vieira de Mello, the accomplished Brazilian diplomat who was now the head of the UN Human Rights Commission. As well as being one of the most skilled and most admired diplomats at the UN, de Mello was one of Annan's closest friends. Vieira de Mello took the job for four months only.

As soon as he arrived in Iraq, Vieira de Mello began to talk to everyone he could, visited as much of Iraq as possible, and flew to different capitals in the area. He saw his task to empower the Iraqis and to get the neighbors to embrace them.

One of the coalition's most important achievements was to create the Iraqi Governing Council in July. Vieira de Mello was crucial in helping to find and persuade the right people to join it. The Governing Council was one of the most broadly based institutions in the entire Arab world—it represented Shia, Sunni, Kurds, Assyrians, Turcomen, and others. There were three women among the twenty-five members—at 12 percent not as high as liberal idealists would like, but rather better than in most of the Arab world.

The Governing Council was praised by Iraqi human rights groups for its transparency. It was responsible for appointing and dismissing ministers and supervising their work. Many (not all) of the ministers it appointed in September were graduates of foreign universities and were far more accomplished than the servile apparatchiks through whom Saddam had ruled for decades.

The second task, persuading neighbors to accept the new Iraq, was the hardest. However much they hated and feared Saddam, there was little public gratitude to the British and Americans for liberating Iraq. To most of the Arab media, the mass graves, the torture chambers, the children's prisons, and the other horrors that were unearthed almost daily in liberated Iraq in April and May seemed to create little impression. Almost no Arab leader or intellectual accepted that a vile regime that killed other Arabs had been removed. Instead, in Egypt there was a new hit song, "Better Saddam's Hell Than America's Paradise." The Arab media were unremittingly hostile to almost everything that happened in the new Iraq.

Indeed, the new authorities in Baghdad later accused the Arab satellite TV network Al-Jazeera of inciting violence. An Iraqi request to have a channel on an Arabic satellite was denied. So the only news that Iraqis could receive was aggressively hostile to their new state.

The familiar reflexive anti-Americanism also informed many Western intellectuals' reaction to the war. For those with a hate-America-first view of the world, there was no saving grace to be found in the deposition of Saddam and the attempt to bring the rules of civil society to the Middle East. One might have expected otherwise from liberal newspapers and the *bien pensants* of the Western world, but no, their conventional wisdoms prevailed.

When it appeared that the National Museum had been ransacked by looters after the fall of Baghdad the Americans were denounced for allowing one of the greatest acts of cultural vandalism ever. Later it transpired that instead of thousands of priceless pieces being stolen, only a few dozen had disappeared—bad enough but not the catastrophe that America's critics had claimed.

Corrections, if they were made, were almost invisible. The *Guardian* splashed across its front page an account of a conversation that Colin Powell and Jack Straw were alleged to have had at the Waldorf in New York in December in which they cast doubt on the evidence of weapons of mass destruction. When Straw showed that he had not even been in New York at the time and no such conversation had ever taken place, a tiny correction appeared on page 25.

Gore Vidal, constantly lauded as the grand old man of liberal letters, dismissed what he called "the Bush-Cheney junta." Asked how the Iraqis could have been liberated from Saddam without the help of the United States, he replied with lofty disdain, "Don't you think that's their problem? That's not your problem, and that's not my problem. There are many bad regimes on earth, we can list several hundred, at the moment I would put the Bush regime as one of them."

One difference between the "bad regimes" that Vidal airily compared to the U.S. administration was that George Bush would soon have to put himself up for reelection—and might very well not win. But people like Vidal found it impossible to acknowledge that thanks to George Bush 23 million Iraqis now had hope.

Tariq Ali, a popular provocateur of British intellectual society, wrote of the "decolonization" of Iraq by the United States and "its bloodshot British adjutant." He hoped they would be driven from the country and that their Iraqi collaborators "may meet the fate of former Iraqi Prime Minister Nuri Said before them." This was an amazing thing to wish for. Nuri Said was the last relatively decent leader of Iraq; he was pro-Western, and he was murdered in a military coup in 1958. His overthrow led to revolving-door coups in which thousands of people were slaughtered over the next few years. Yet Tariq Ali has seemed to desire that such bloodshed be visited on all those Iraqis who took the opportunity that the United States had given them to create a better country.

Up came Margaret Drabble, celebrated British novelist, calling for pity in the *Daily Telegraph*, less than a month after Saddam's overthrow. "I knew that the wave of anti-Americanism that would swell up after the Iraq war would make me feel ill. And it has. It has made me much, much more ill than I had expected. My anti-Americanism has become almost uncontrollable.... I now loathe the United States and what it has done to Iraq and the rest of the helpless world."

What the United States has done to Iraq? At the time Drabble was writing, the United States had freed Iraq from one of the most monstrous tyrannies of the twenty-first century. As Drabble was writing in London, Iraqi women and children were scrabbling through the dirt of the latest mass grave to be found, searching desperately for the remains of relatives murdered by Saddam. At the same time, the coalition had enacted human rights legislation to ensure that Iraqis would never again be abused in that way.

The famous British playwright Sir David Hare published a diatribe against Bush and Blair. He claimed that Britain and American had decided to "annex" Iraq. He described Britain as "more whore than racketeer" and declared that "it is now impossible to imagine any American foreign policy, however irrational, however dangerous, however illegal, with which our present prime minister would not declare himself publicly delighted and thrilled."

His complaints did not make even the slightest nod to the tragic nature of the decisions that governments must take in the post-9/11 world. In Hare's diatribe there was much sorrow that his views were not taken seriously enough, but there was not a word about what the Iraqi people had suffered for decades.

Contempt of America sometimes mingled with conspiracy. Michael Meacher, a former Labour minister, opined that 9/11 was all an American plot. After describing wrongly U.S. air movements on that day, he asked: "Was this inaction simply the result of key people disregarding or being ignorant of the evidence? Or could U.S. air security operations have been deliberately stood down on September 11? If so, why, and on whose authority?" Whose indeed?

Fortunately there were other voices. John Burns of the *New York Times*, had been one of the most courageous journalists to work under Saddam. Unlike many others he had not trimmed to suit the regime. After the war was over, Burns criticized those foreign correspondents who ignored how "Saddam had turned his country into a slaughterhouse." After the fall of Saddam, ingratiating letters from one of the BBC's star correspondents were found in the files of the Foreign Ministry. He was not alone. Burns complained that reporters sucked up to the Minister of Information, wining and dining him, "plying him with mobile phones at $600 each for members of his family, and giving bribes of thousands of dollars." Such journalists then "behaved as if they were in Belgium. They never mentioned the function of minders. Never mentioned terror."

Some French intellectuals and public figures like Bernard Kouchner, the founder of Medecins Sans Frontiers, Andre Glucksman, and Bernard Henri Levy defended the rights of the Iraqi people to be free. Ann Clywd, a left-wing British member of Parliament, had campaigned for years for the Iraqi people and now supported the British and American governments. Christopher Hitchens, a prolific English writer and the scourge of Henry Kissinger, celebrated the overthrow of Saddam with consistent panache. In London John Lloyd, writer and now an editor on the *Financial Times*, made it his job to draw attention to some of the more outrageous assaults on America. He published a critical analysis by the historian Ian Buruma of the rhetoric that I noted above from Gore Vidal, Tariq Ali, and others. Buruma himself had doubted the reasons for war going to war in Iraq, but he asked: "Why are our left-liberal intellectuals so hopeless at answering [the] vital question . . . of what to do, as citizens of the richest and most powerful nations on earth, about dictators who commit mass murder or happily starve millions to death?" He wondered why for so many of these people a visceral loathing of America was so important that they simply could not see that many Iraqis might be glad to be rid of Saddam's people-shredders.

The critics of course had a field day when it became clear that the allies could not quickly find weapons of mass destructions. Among the prowar allies, many different reasons had been given to explain the need for war. In the United States, President Bush had insisted that Iraq had supported terrorism (as it had, even if there was little evidence of direct involvement with Al Qaeda), that after 9/11 America could not tolerate outlaw states accumulating weapons of mass destruction in defiance of the world. In Britain, by contrast, Tony Blair had hewed to the strict line that Britain was justified in enforcing UN resolutions that Saddam disarm or suffer "serious consequences." For Blair, therefore, the discovery of the weapons was more important than it was for Bush.

By late summer 2003 no such weapons had been found in Iraq. Blair's critics on both the right and the left began to accuse him of misleading the British public and taking the country to war to counter a threat that did not exist. The problem for Blair was that whereas George Bush had always thought that regime change as such was a good enough reason for attacking Saddam, Blair had always insisted on the legal cover provided by Iraq's flouting of successive UN resolutions and possession of proscribed weapons of mass destruction.

At the end of May 2003 a BBC reporter, Andrew Gilligan, alleged that an official had told him that the intelligence services were unhappy because Downing Street had deliberately "sexed up" its September 2002 dossier on Saddam's weapons. Specifically he claimed that the government probably knew that its claim that Iraq's WMD could be launched in 45 minutes was false. The official was later revealed to be David Kelly, an excellent weapons expert but not an intelligence officer. Under mounting public pressure, Dr. Kelly apparently committed suicide. Evidence given to the public inquiry into his tragic death showed that while the original BBC claim had been untrue, some intelligence officials (but not their superiors) had been uneasy that parts of the dossier had exaggerated Saddam's WMD threat.

It is worth recalling that the British and American governments were not alone in insisting that Saddam retained WMD. In Resolution 1441 of November 2002 every single member of the Security Council voted that Saddam had still failed to account for his illegal weapons and demanded that he disarm. In his various appearances before the Security Council up to the moment of war, Hans Blix was cautious and questioned some American allegations, but he too said that Iraq had failed to account for missing weapons or systems.

Further support for Blair and Bush came from other weapons experts. At the end of June Richard Spertzel, the head of UNSCOM's biological weapons section from 1994 to 1999, insisted that that there was no doubt that Iraq had had a biological weapons program. Rolf Ekeus, the Swedish diplomat who had been the first head of UNSCOM in the 1990s, argued that criticism of Bush and Blair over the failure to find the weapons "is a distortion and trivialization of a major threat to international peace and security."

Ekeus argued that Iraqi policy since 1991 was not to produce warfare agents but rather to concentrate on design and engineering "with the purpose of activating production and shipping of warfare agents and munitions directly to the battlefield in the event of war." Much of this work was done in ordinary civilian facilities. "This combination of researchers, engineers, know-how, precursors, batch production techniques is what constituted Iraq's chemical threat—its chemical weapons." Not rusting drums.

Now that Saddam was no longer a threat to the region, there was at last a possibility of reshaping the Middle East and the Persian Gulf into areas that brought more peace and stability to their populations. "This is enough to justify the international military intervention undertaken by the United States and Britain," said Ekeus. "To accept the alternative—letting Hussein remain in power—would have been to tolerate a continuing destabilizing arms race in the Gulf, including future nuclearization of the region, threats to the world's energy supplies, leakage of WMD technology and expertise to terrorist networks, systematic sabotage of efforts to create and sustain a process of peace between the Israelis and the Palestinians and the continued terrorizing of the Iraqi people."

The official U.S. search was in the hands of the Iraq Survey Group, under the former UN weapons inspector David Kay. In early October Kay's group published its interim report. It was a careful document; the group could not prove the American and British belief that Iraqi WMD had been an "immediate" threat. It found no massive stockpile of illegal weapons that could have been used against the invading forces or against other states.

But the report did show the elaborate efforts to which Saddam had gone to destroy evidence, disperse material, and confuse and even threaten searchers. Files had been burned, computer hard drives destroyed. People were taking potshots at the team. The report pointed out that "even the bulkiest materials we are looking for, in the quantities we could expect to find, can be concealed in a space not much larger than a two-car garage."

It was easy for critics of the war to claim that the report showed they had been right all along and there was never any WMD to justify the invasion. It is true that Kay and his search teams had not discovered an illegally improved, extended-range Al-Husseini missile loaded with anthrax or VX gas. There were no vast stockpiles of weapons ready to fire, and so the enemies of Bush and Blair instantly declared that the war was a fraud.

But the report in fact made for frightening reading. It demonstrated that Saddam had continued to violate Security Council resolutions long after the inspectors were obliged to leave in 1998, that there was an organized strategy of deception, and that there was serious evidence that Iraq was still trying to obtain biological and chemical weapons. On biological warfare, debriefings and site visits "have begun to unravel a clandestine network of laboratories and facilities within the security service apparatus. This network was never declared to the UN and was previously unknown." It was clear that Iraq concealed equipment and materials from the inspectors when they returned in 2002.

Kay said he found a prison laboratory complex possibly used in human testing of biological weapons agents that had not been revealed to the UN. He discovered much other research programming that had been concealed from the inspectors.

One problem in the search for chemical weapons was the proverbial haystack. Kay's men and women had to contend with the "almost unbelievable scale" of Iraq's armory of conventional weapons. There were some 130 ammunition storage points, some of them more than fifty square miles in size. So far the group had had time to examine only ten of these depots. The Iraqi practice was to hide chemical shells among the conventional rounds—and altogether Kay reckoned there were about 600,000 tons of shells, rockets, and bombs to sort through.

On nuclear weapons, Kay became convinced from the interviews he conducted that Saddam was still committed to acquiring them. Iraqi officials "assert that Saddam would have resumed nuclear weapons development at some future point. Some indicated a resumption after Iraq was free of sanctions." His delivery systems were also being constantly (and illegally) improved. According to interviews, Saddam had ordered the development of ballistic missiles with a range between 400 and 1,000 kilometers. Measures to conceal these projects from UNMOVIC were initiated in late 2002, ahead of the arrival of inspectors.

The heart of the matter was that Kay stated that Saddam had not given up on trying to acquire WMD. "We have discovered dozens of WMD related program activities and significant amounts if equipment that Iraq concealed from the United Nations during the inspections that began in late 2002."

It was quite clear that he intended to resume the programs "whenever the external restrictions were removed"—for example, if sanctions had been lifted. Several officials they had interviewed had been asked by Saddam or his sons since 2000 "about how long it would take to either restart [chemical weapons] production or make available chemical weapons." Moreover, if the United States had not overthrown Saddam, he would have continued to develop missiles with a range of 1,000 kilometers—far more than the 150 kilometers permitted Iraq by the UN.

Kay asked for more time to continue the search on the grounds first that the empirical reality in the field would certainly be different from intelligence assessments. Proliferation of WMD was such a continuing threat to the world that it was necessary to learn those lessons. Second, "we have found people, technical information, and illicit procurement networks that if allowed to flow to other countries and regions could accelerate global proliferation."

The Kay report did not show that Iraq had been an immediate threat. But it did provide irrefutable evidence that Saddam's WMD ambitions were an inevitable threat.

Kay showed that Saddam had deliberately defied Resolution 1441, unanimously passed by the Security Council, which had demanded that he make a full accounting of his WMD and warned that there would be no more tolerance for concealment and obstruction. Both Blair and Bush argued that the decision to go to war had been vindicated by Kay's findings. Bush asked Congress to make a massive new sum, $600 million, available to continue the search.

If it was hard to follow the progress of the weapons inspectors, it was even more difficult to understand the real progress of Iraq during the summer of 2003. In Europe and the United States headlines described the worsening security problems for U.S. troops in particular. President Bush had been ill-advised when he swooped down, in full military dress, onto the deck of an aircraft carrier on May 1 to declare "Mission Accomplished" and that major combat operations were over. There was much that still needed to be completed.

A senior British military analyst (and former intelligence official) who spent six weeks in Baghdad in the summer was discouraged and discouraging. He thought the CPA was "geriatric" and spent far too much time in its compound. Momentum had been lost, the whole operation was underfunded, and very little cash was finding its way into the ministries where it was needed. Officials, he said, seemed to have been selected only for their loyalty to Donald Rumsfeld. The Iraqi army had been disbanded too hastily, and out-of-work soldiers were now a serious threat. U.S. troops were undertrained (too many reservists) and overstretched. Also, 60 percent of the U.S. armored division in the city was on guard duty. No wonder morale was low.

By the summer of 2003, the security situation had worsened, especially for U.S. troops. British and American headlines described the horror of the new Iraq. It was difficult to be optimistic. But the gory stories in the Western media did not reflect the reality for most of the population. In the Sunni Triangle north of Baghdad where the Saddamite revanchists and others were concentrated, violence seemed to be endemic and growing.

However, on July 22 the lure of a $15 million reward led to the betrayal of Saddam's two loyal sons, Uday and Qusay. They were tracked to a house in the town of Mosul; after a violent siege the two men were killed. This was a welcome success for the coalition and a reminder of the exquisite horrors of the regime it had overthrown. Uday, the elder son, was a particularly terrible person. His obituary in *The Times* described him as "one of the most notorious and obnoxious men in the history of the Middle East."

Qusay was a more sophisticated and efficient killer. Each man represented aspects of his father perfectly. There cannot have been many people in the world who mourned either of them.

The Americans had hoped that their deaths would diminish the strength of the Saddamite resistance. But the man of darkness, Saddam himself, remained elusive, and until he was captured or killed his supporters would continue to fight for a restoration. Nor were the revanchists of the old regime alone. Islamic fundamentalists were pouring across the Syrian and other borders into Iraq; they would hardly notice the death of Saddam; they certainly would not see it as a reason to desist in their assaults upon the infidel.

Paul Bremer said that much of the violence being carried out in late summer 2003 was by fighters from Ansar al-Islam, a terrorist group with links to Al Qaeda that the United States had tried to destroy. Before the war they had been based in the Kurdish zones; many of them had escaped into Iran during the war and then crossed back into Iraq. Just as Afghanistan had attracted the mujahideen to fight the infidels in the 1980s, so Iraq was inspiring a new generation of young Muslim fighters.

They were well-organized. One group of Ansar al-Islam captured in the Kurdish region at the end of July consisted of five Iraqis, a Palestinian, and a Tunisian. They were carrying five forged Italian passports for another group of terrorists, according to Neil MacFarquhar of the *New York Times*.

It was virtually impossible to stop such people crossing Iraq's frontiers. Indeed, neighboring states connived in their entry into Iraq, hoping to destroy the Anglo-American administration there. Bremer told Michael Gordon of the *New York Times*, "The intelligence suggests at Ansar al-Islam is planning large scale terrorist attacks here. So long as we have, as I think we do, substantial numbers of Ansar terrorists around here, I think we have to be pretty alert to the fact that we may see more of this."

He was right. Iraq was now seen by some Islamists as an epic opportunity. Mullah Mustapha Kreikar, the spiritual leader of Ansar al-Islam, in exile in Norway, told an Arab satellite channel that the fight against the Americans in Iraq was the same as that against the Soviets in Afghanistan. Echoing the warnings of Bernard Lewis, he said, "The resistance is not only a reaction to the American invasion, it's part of the continuous Islamic struggle since the collapse of the caliphate. All Islamic struggles since then are part of one organized effort to bring back the caliphate."

In August the terror campaign against the occupiers and those who were seen as helping them increased in ferocity and destructiveness. Most attacks on U.S. troops had been by rocket-propelled grenades, explosive devices, and small arms. Suddenly the tactics changed, for the worse.

On 14 August a car bomb exploded outside the Jordanian embassy, killing seventeen people and wounding many more. Then on August 19 the United Nations was attacked.

In all twenty-two people were killed and many more horribly wounded (see the Introduction). Apart from Vieira de Mello himself, the UN lost many other fine people because they had sent their "A team" to Baghdad.

The shock to the UN system was great; never before had the UN been attacked in this way. A subsequent report, commissioned by Kofi Annan, showed UN security in Baghdad to have been inadequate. Vieira de Mello and others had thought that the UN's neutrality would help protect it. Not in this world. It was a terrible blow for Annan personally. "We are dealing with really, really bad people who have no value for their lives," he said to me of the bombers. "And therefore no value for the lives of others. They will do anything for their cause, to create chaos."

Annan said at first that the UN would remain in Iraq, but he was faced with a virtual rebellion among those in the Secretariat. Within weeks the UN pulled out almost all its people. That was bad for the UN and for Iraq. It was good for nihilists who wished to destroy the chance for the Iraqi people to progress.

More was to come. In the most obvious attempt to destabilize the Shiite majority of Iraq, one of the most important Shiite clerics, Ayatollah Mohammed Baqir al-Hakim, was assassinated by a car bomb in Najaf on August 28. The ayatollah's family had been persecuted, and many of them murdered, by Saddam. He had fled to Iran and felt able to return to Iraq only after the overthrow of Saddam. His homecoming in Najaf was triumphant, and he instantly became one of the leaders of the Shia community.

He had advocated caution and cooperation rather than resistance to the American rulers. Who killed him? Almost certainly Baathists or Sunni Arabs who were frightened of the rise of Shia power or a more radical Shia faction that opposed his cooperation with the occupiers. In the event the Shia community remained remarkably calm.

The next high-profile attack was on Akila al-Hashemi, a female member of the Iraqi Governing Council who was gunned down outside her house as she was preparing to go to represent Iraq at the United Nations. Annan said that "such murderous use of violence is wholly inexcusable, and likely only to retard the process of establishing a broad-based and representative government in Iraq, to which sovereignty can be transferred."

★

Nothing can diminish the horror of all these killings, or the real possibility that if they are not stopped the aim of the murderers to create chaos could succeed. But behind the violence there was another story. One of steady rebuilding, both of the physical infrastructure and of institutions.

In Baghdad by August 2003, the crack and thrum of weapons fire was mingled with the roar of jackhammers rebuilding streets, homes, shops. Vivienne Walt, an American journalist, wrote compellingly of the two levels of life—war and reconstruction—that were taking place. "It may seem strange, but this city is suddenly throbbing with street life, even as the guerrilla insurgency drags on." The roads were jammed with brand-new BMWs and Mercedes sedans driven straight over from the Gulf states. The telephones still didn't work, but Internet cafes were everywhere. Given the long nightmare of controls and commands from which the city had been awoken, the progress toward a free economy was rather astonishing.

Walt quoted people's exasperation with the nervous and dangerous American troops patrolling the streets. They certainly were not popular in the city. But Iraqis she talked to had a sense of things getting better. The polls showed the same. Polling is a new phenomenon in Iraq. Ordinary Iraqis found it astonishing suddenly to be asked what they thought. No one gave a damn about their views under Saddam—unless of course they expressed thoughts that were at variance with the orders of the president.

Now people found themselves for the first time being asked their opinions. All the polls that were conducted showed that the vast majority of people were glad that the allies had overthrown Saddam Hussein. They might resent the lack of security and the slowness with which the country was being repaired, but they were optimistic for the future. One common feeling was that people expected to be better off five years hence. Only a small minority wanted the coalition to leave at once.

Utilities were still a problem. They had been bad before the invasion. Iraq had never produced enough power even for Baghdad. Saddam used to forcibly black out other cities to keep the lights on in the capital. But by September 39,000 electricity workers were back at work, bringing Basra power 24/7 for the first time since 1991 and Baghdad for about eighteen hours a day. Power generation was higher that at any time since the war began. Kuwait had delivered seven out of eight power generators committed as part of an aid package. The Iraqi Ministry of Health was spending $40 million on 128 generators for hospitals. Lines for gasoline had ended, and garbage was being collected again.

According to the British government, by September

Baghdad was receiving 80 percent of its prewar water supply. The Baghdad sewage system was still not repaired. All twelve Baghdad hospitals were operational, though some still faced serious problems. They were all short of supplies—but they had been before the invasion, when Saddam had diverted so much of the money and materiel meant for health care into building his palaces.

The United States had been much too slow in recognizing the need for a civilian police force. Police should have come into the country immediately after Saddam's defeat. The U.S. Army was simply unable to carry out police work effectively.

By October, a police force was just beginning to take shape. Bernard Kerik had spent four months trying to set it up. The task was to set up an entirely new force with training in human rights as well as discipline. "We had to teach cops," he wrote later, "that when you pull a man suspected of a crime into the station, you can't just hang him upside down and beat him with an iron bar."

By September some 40,000 police officers had been trained (at least somewhat). A force of at least double that was needed. Kerik says that thirty-five police stations were set up in Baghdad while he was there. "Try setting up thirty-five stations in New York in four months." It took Mayor Rudolph Giuliani eight years to create a safe city out of

New York, Kerik pointed out. As well as the civil police, there were 2,750 border police, 12,500 Facilities Protection Service personnel, and 4,500 members of the Civil Defence Corps. Yet critics argued that in Kosovo the United States had led a more substantial and integrated effort to create a decent police after NATO's invasion. A police academy had been created there. Less effort had so far been made in Iraq.

Nonetheless, to the bombers the new police force seemed a clear threat—they attacked its members brutally. On October 9 a car bomber careened into a police station in Baghdad, killing eight new officers and wounding more than forty people.

Civil society was being rebuilt—slowly, of course. There was a completely free press; anyone could receive satellite broadcasts, even if almost all the Arab broadcasts, reflecting their masters' voices, remained irremediably hostile to the new Iraq reality. Dozens of newspapers had been set up, each catering to a different section of the population. There were Sunni, Shia, and Kurdish papers and papers catering to democrats, communists, and Islamists. By September all Iraqi cities and most towns had working municipal councils. Baghdad had nine municipal councils that worked together well. New professional associations were being created; old ones suppressed by Saddam were being restored.

There was still a lot of unemployment, but jobs were

increasing with wages and salaries. Food prices were lower than before. Shops that had been empty for years were now stuffed with imported goods. It was like Ali Baba's cave—everything that had been denied Iraqis in the long years of Saddam and sanctions was suddenly available. Currency reform was being pushed through, the banking system was reviving, the great trading families were cautiously putting money back into the country from which they had been forcibly detached so long, and in the 80 percent of the country not being terrorized business was restoring itself fast. Property prices were increasing even in Baghdad, where the Court of First Instance was creating procedures to resolve disputes over debts, landlord problems, and property confiscated during the Saddam regime. And the stock market was coming back to life.

It might not have been clear to all foreign journalists and intellectuals, but it was clear to an assessment mission from the UN National Democratic Institute (NDI) what was happening. "NDI's overwhelming finding—in the north, south, Baghdad, and among secular, religious, Sunni, Shiite and Kurdish groups in both urban and rural areas—is a grateful welcoming of the demise of Saddam's regime and a sense that this is a pivotal moment in Iraq's history."

Oil production was increasing, though at 1.9 million barrels per day it was still down from prewar levels. So far oil had earned the country about $1.6 billion, and the CPA said that revenues ought to be almost $5 billion for the year—more than the target. They hoped to reopen the pipeline to Turkey, recently blown up by saboteurs, by mid-October. But the airport remained closed because of the threat of ground-to-air missiles, hundreds of which had disappeared when Saddam's army melted away in April.

In early October schools reopened. About 1,100 looted schools around the country were reported to have been restored. There was the delightful sight of children walking along streets in uniforms and carrying new satchels. For the first time the children would not be taught of the glory of Saddam.

Emblematic of the improvements was that the Marsh Arabs, whose rivers had been drained by Saddam, began to get their water back. Soon after the U.S. victory, Iraqi engineers opened lock gates on the Euphrates, allowing the water to spill once more into the lands that the Marsh Arabs had inhabited for centuries. The flow of water was not as strong as it used to be, but by early fall some of the marshes had been reflooded. The *Washington Post* reported, "As the blanket of water gradually expands, it is quickly nourishing plants, animals and a way of life for Marsh Arabs that Hussein tried so assiduously to extinguish."

Julie Flint, a correspondent of the *Observer*, wrote in early

October that things were going much better than most journalists wished to claim. She quoted a university lecturer, whose colleagues had been burned to death, as saying, "I feel as if I had been born again. Iraq was a prison above ground and a mass grave beneath it." She wrote that it was nonsense to suggest that there was an Iraqi popular resistance to the British and Americans. The violence was being caused "by the very people most Iraqis reject—the remnants of Saddam's Baath party and extremists flooding in from neighboring countries in hope of establishing religious rule. They, not the liberators/occupiers, are the real threat to peace in Iraq and stability in the wider region today."

But among the old allies the old enmities flared again. France decided to lead the charge against U.S. control of Iraq by demanding a swift timetable for the handover of power to an Iraqi provisional government. This call was echoed by the United Nations, still reeling from the terrible attack on its office in Baghdad and the loss of Sergio Vieira de Mello and so many others.

Dominique de Villepin rejected the U.S. call for broader UN-based help in Iraq unless the United States handed over all authority. President Bush proposed that past quarrels between the allies should now be set aside in the interests

of Iraq. But it was clear that the quarrels were being
reignited. France and Germany rejected a draft U.S. resolution put forward in early September that retained overall
U.S. command and political authority while the Governing
Council prepared a constitution, elections, and self-rule.

Instead France demanded that the United States surrender power in Iraq much more quickly and completely if it
was to receive any help from France and its allies. De
Villepin was scornful of U.S. problems—he seemed almost
to be willing that the United States fail in Iraq. He attacked
neoconservatives for thinking "in a framework of yester-
day's world, especially on the issue of power." He and
Jacques Chirac became so aggressive that *New York Times*
columnist Thomas Friedman, who had followed Iraq
closely, asserted that France was no longer an annoying ally
or a jealous rival: "France is becoming America's enemy."

Acknowledging the mistakes made by the Bush administration, Friedman said that if France really cared for the
future of Iraq, it would be trying to assemble 25,000
"Eurotroops" and a huge financial package for the country.
"But then France has never been interested in promoting
democracy in the modern Arab world, which is why its
pose as the new protector of Iraqi representative government—after being so content with Saddam's one-man
rule—is so patently cynical."

The French, backed though not fully by the Germans, claimed that internationalizing the forces and the governance of Iraq would diminish the violent opposition to it. This was hard to understand. Some 80 percent of the population (including most Shia and most Kurds) were pleased to see the end of their persecutor, Saddam. The only group that was thoroughly opposed to the change were the Sunni minority, which Saddam had elevated and which had oppressed fellow citizens for so long. They would fight anyone to retain their hold on power—even Frenchmen, if they saw them as standing in the way of restoring Saddam, which, to be fair, not even the French were proposing. Neither France nor Germany could easily find even 5,000 troops to send to Iraq to join the 140,000 Americans, 10,000 British, 9,000 Poles, and others—even if Chirac had wished to do so.

To the British and Americans it seemed that the sudden handover of power being pushed by the French and Germans was self-serving, impractical, unwise, and dangerous. It was a recipe for increasing chaos and the power of the fundamentalists.

It was hard to find Iraqis in any position of responsibility who agreed with the French timetable. Nor did anyone have real confidence that troops from Bangladesh or Indonesia, for example, would succeed in playing the role of UN peacekeepers in Iraq. They had found Kosovo hard enough—this was more dangerous and much more complicated.

Why should such speed be forced upon Iraq? The UN had occupied Bosnia for seven years before giving the locals power; it has been occupying Kosovo for four years; and Sergio Vieira de Mello had ruled East Timor for two years before the territory won its independence.

All these places—particularly tiny East Timor, half an island with a homogenous population of less than 1 million—were far, far simpler than Iraq. Even the horrors of ethnic cleansing in Bosnia and Kosovo were nothing compared to the horrors of genocide, mass murder, and mayhem visited on Iraq by decades of tyranny from Saddam's rule and by those who sought to create chaos in his absence.

Moreover, even if all were peace and harmony, there were six times as many Iraqis as Bosnians, more than twenty-three times as many Iraqis as East Timorese. How could transfer of power possibly be achieved more quickly in Iraq than in such places?

The French suddenly invested great faith in the Governing Council. This was odd since the French and the Germans had refused to endorse the body when it was set up two months earlier. They had dismissed its members as American puppets.

The Governing Council was an important step toward creating a new Iraqi civil society, but in summer 2003 it could not be transformed overnight into a government. At worst, the French proposal sounded almost like a desperately cynical attempt to make sure that the "Anglo-Saxon" attempt to create a better Iraq was bound to fail.

The Americans and the British favored moving directly to an elected Iraqi government by the end of 2004, rather than creating a provisional government in the meantime. One unknown was how long the constitutional process would take. It was the Council's task to decide how to write a new constitution for the country. This would not be easy. First, how was a constituent assembly to be created? Members of the council did not want it to be appointed by the British and Americans, but nor were elections possible in the current situation. The assembly would have huge decisions to make: the status of the Kurdish region, the role of Islam in the constitution, and whether the country should have a presidential or parliamentary system. All are hard questions.

Iraqi society needed a healing process after the horrors of Saddam. An immediate transfer of power in fall 2003, as proposed by the French and now underwritten by the United Nations, still reeling from its loss, could reverse this. New political leaders would try to use the instruments of the new state to enforce their grip. The experiences of recent years in Bosnia, Kosovo, and Afghanistan showed how enduringly difficult it is to force democratic changes on societies that have been schooled in repression, let alone tyranny.

Fareed Zakaria described the dilemma well when he said that popular sovereignty was great but constitutional process greater still. "The French know this. The French Revolution emphasized popular sovereignty with little regard to limitations on state power. The American founding, by contrast, was obsessed with constitution-making. Both countries got to genuine democracy. But in France it took two centuries, five republics, two empires, and one dictatorship to get there. Surely we want to do it better in Iraq?"

The debate at the United Nations turned nasty by the end of September. The French and Germans tried to obstruct progress toward a new resolution that was satisfactory to everyone. The casuistry of French officials, in particular Jacques Chirac and Dominique de Villepin, was sometimes breathtaking. The *London Times* editorialized, "France appears to be gloating over America's difficulties, all too evident in the daily toll of deaths in terrorist attacks on US forces. These forces are trying to bring order to a country emerging from decades of dictatorship and conflict, and yet that honourable aim is treated with contempt by Paris."

In mounting frustration, State Department officials said they might withdraw America's draft resolution and drop the attempt to seek any further authorization by the Council.

The deadlock was broken by President Putin, who decided in mid-October to abandon the French and Germans and back the Anglo-American position. On October 16 the Council voted unanimously to approve Resolution 1551. It recognized the legitimacy of the Provisional Authority and thus of regime change. It endorsed the U.S.-led multinational force. In return, Washington formally acknowledged that its interest in running Iraq was only temporary. Resolution 1551 empowered the United Nations to expand its political, economic, and humanitarian activities in Iraq and called upon the UN to assist the Governing Council with setting up a constitutional conference.

Resolution 1551 was an important step forward. But France and its partners still refused to acknowledge that the creation of a new Iraq is one of the most pressing international challenges of our time. At the Madrid conference in October, commitments of $13 billion over five years were made toward the reconstruction of Iraq. At the same time the United States was expected to offer Iraq some $20 billion. The Arab states offered very little, and the European Union and European states together came through with only $800 million. France and Germany offered nothing. Chris Patten, the EU's Commissioner for External Affairs, claimed that the European contribution was "realistic." Iraqis in the interim government who traveled to Madrid thought by contrast that it was measly and seemed to reflect instead that the European Union did not have a real interest in helping to bring a better order to Iraq and the Middle East.

Chapter 6

THE RIGHT THING TO DO

THE UNITED STATES, Britain, Austrailia, Spain, Poland, and their coalition partners took enormous risks when they invaded Iraq in March 2003.

In fact, they risked one of the most successful alliances in history. They risked damaging the United Nations, not to mention themselves, by first seeking a new Security Council resolution and then going to war after they had failed to secure it. They risked diverting resources from the struggle with Al Qaeda, which had taken such urgent form on September 11, 2001.

They risked a much bloodier war, one in which they feared chemical or biological weapons might be used against their troops. Perhaps most dangerous of all, they risked creating a new swamp in which terrorists could actually breed and flourish. But they were clear that these and other risks had to be taken.

Retreat in the face of the French veto would have presented greater risks. It would have left Saddam triumphant,
all the more able to terrorize his own people and threaten
the region. American power would have been immeasur-
ably weakened. America's friends would no longer be able
to depend on it, while its enemies would know that it could
be faced down. It would have made the United Nations
redundant—its resolutions would no longer have any force
if such a clearly criminal violator of its resolutions as Saddam could not be held to account. It would have sent a
message to all rogue states—let alone the other two members of the "axis of evil," Iran and North Korea—that there
was actually nothing to stop them from acquiring nuclear
weapons.

The threat from Saddam was well described by President Bill Clinton back in February 1998, another time of
crisis caused by Saddam's refusal to obey the Security
Council. Since so many Europeans like to contrast President George W. Bush's attitude to Iraq unfavorably to that
of Clinton, it is worth quoting the former president at
some length.

"Now let's imagine the future," Clinton said.

What if he fails to comply and we fail to act, or we take
some ambiguous third route, which gives him yet more

opportunities to develop this program of weapons of mass destruction and continue to press for the release of the sanctions and continue to ignore the solemn commitments he has made? Well, he will conclude that the international community has lost its will. He will then conclude that he can go right on and do more to rebuild an arsenal of devastating destruction. And some day, some way, I guarantee you he'll use the arsenal....

In the next century, the community of nations may see more and more of the very kind of threat Iraq poses now—a rogue state with weapons of mass destruction, ready to use them or provide them to terrorists, drug traffickers, or organized criminals who travel the world among us unnoticed.

If we fail to respond today, Saddam, and all those who would follow in his footsteps, will be emboldened tomorrow by the knowledge that they can act with impunity, even in the face of a clear message from the United Nations Security Council, and clear evidence of a weapons of mass destruction program.

Clinton was absolutely right. But caught in the uproar over the Monica Lewinsky crisis, he failed to follow though. That was left to Bush.

★

Hindsight is a wonderful thing. But it is clear that mistakes were made and are still being made by the allies in Iraq.

It was a mistake for Tony Blair to rely so much in his public case on intelligence findings on weapons of mass destruction. He wanted to prove to his own Labour Party and his skeptical European neighbors that Saddam's WMD program was a real threat—since the dictator's record of torturing and gassing his own people, of invading his neighbors, of financing suicide bombers, and of mocking the rule of law as written over twelve years by the United Nations was not motivation enough for domestic liberal elites. But the end result was a case that proved less than absolute: After the war, when uncovering WMD proved much more elusive than the U.S. and British governments had predicted, public trust in the strategy for Iraq was diminished.

Similarly, the turf wars in Washington have been unhelpful in the vital task of reconstructing Iraq as a humane modern society. The CIA's refusal to enlist more Iraqis in the coalition at the start made it much harder to explain its purpose to the Iraqi people. The Pentagon's early insistence on total control of reconstruction and its failure to prepare for that role were lamentable. The dissonance on aims and methods between the State Department and the Pentagon, and the inability of Condoleezza Rice,

the national security adviser, or even President Bush himself, to impose policy contributed to the problem.

It was a mistake not to inform the Iraqi people better of
the coalition's intentions. Radio stations should have been
pumping out the message that the United States was coming to help, not to steal Iraq's oil any more than it had
stolen Kuwait's oil after liberation in 1991.

The coalition did not anticipate the extent and the
sophistication of the guerrilla attacks that would follow
victory in the formal military campaign. They did not
expect the Saddam elite to melt away with hundreds of
millions of stolen dollars to finance constant brutal attacks
upon coalition forces and Iraqis working with them.

It was a mistake not to do more to close the borders
with Iran and Syria to stop the flood of Islamic terrorists
pouring into Iraq.

Since the end of the war questions have once again been
raised as to its legality. Lawyers will always argue; they are
well paid to do that. And so it is worth remembering the
legal basis of the war: Quite apart from the legitimate
grounds of self-defense in a new world of proliferating
weapons of mass destruction, it was intended to remove a
regime that had been defined by the Security Council as a
threat to peace and security since 1990, when the Council
passed Resolution 678 after Iraq's invasion of Kuwait.

In March 2003, not one of the fifteen members doubted that Iraq was still in breach of all the relevant, binding Council resolutions since 678. The Council was split, but no new resolution was required to endorse war because the Council had already confirmed its earlier authority to use force for the restoration of peace and security.

George W. Bush could justify telling the UN General Assembly in September 2003 that the United States had enforced Security Council resolutions against Saddam's Iraq. To liberal internationalists the most important task is to preserve the authority of the UN Security Council. They have a point when arguing that the doctrine of pre-emption could lead to the law of the jungle. But unanswered defiance of the Council, as practiced by Saddam for more than a decade, mocks the whole purpose of the United Nations.

The war has provoked an impassioned debate over how international relations should be conducted in the post–9/11 world. This debate is necessary: Since 9/11 the dark ambitions of Islamic terrorism and the proliferation of weapons of mass destruction have forced us to try to chart new diplomatic and ethical territory.

But the debate has not always been conducted in constructive terms within the Western world. Polarization has allowed the protagonists sometimes to avoid their responsibility for achieving agreement in the face of the implacable evil represented by Saddam and bin Laden and those who subscribe to the nihilist ideology of Al Qaeda.

There is wide agreement that the UN has to change to meet the new threats. Charles Powell, who was Margaret Thatcher's foreign policy adviser, says that terrorists "cannot be handled exclusively within the old rules and institutions. A UN system devised in the world of the 1940s needs to be modified. New dangers which threaten our security or promote humanitarian disaster must be caught at an early stage and dealt with even if—after reasonable efforts to achieve consensus—the international community as a whole is not ready to go along."

Kofi Annan, while protecting the authority of the Security Council, agrees that change is essential. In September 2003 he said that the UN had "come to a fork in the road. This may be a moment no less important than 1945 itself when the United Nations was founded."

He criticized the American doctrine of preemption, saying that it represented a fundamental challenge to the principles on which the world tries to maintain peace. But he also said, "It is not enough to denounce unilateralism, unless we also face up squarely to the concerns that make some states feel uniquely vulnerable, since it is those concerns that drive them to take unilateral action. We must show that those concerns can, and will, be addressed effectively through collective action."

Annan knows that the UN's record at changing itself is not encouraging. And the United States is likely to argue that it cannot wait. The Secretary-General realizes that time is very short. "History is a harsh judge; it will not forgive us if we let this moment pass."

In an interview with this author before his speech to the General Assembly, Annan said that he wanted members to come up with ideas on how to make the UN and the world work better. He divided the main threats that the world faces into "hard threats," like weapons of mass destruction and terrorism, and "soft threats," like poverty, deprivation, and AIDS. He thinks many more people around the world feel threatened by the soft threats than the hard ones. And he is right—the West must address those wider threats to the world in addition to the specific threats to itself.

I asked him if he did not think the region (and the world) was not much better off without Saddam. He agreed: "People are happy Saddam has gone, but they had not expected this disorder to follow. If it leads to chaos in the whole region, they will blame the Americans. If we cannot effectively manage the current situation, it could get worse than anything that Saddam, with all his wickedness, could have done." He was concerned that by delaying a handover to the Iraqis, America would miss the curve of events.

It is undoubtedly true that the follow-through of the war is at least as important as the war itself—and much more difficult. American commitment and patience will be badly tried over years, not months. But it has to be a joint effort; that is why the wrecking tactics of President Chirac's government throughout 2003 have been so cynical, so counterproductive, and so destructive. And France's ambition, endorsed by many senior EU officials, that Europe should make itself a "counterweight" or rival to the United States is a vanity, a delusion that can only weaken the defenses of the world.

Tony Blair spelled out today's realities in a speech to a joint session of the U.S. Congress in July 2003. "The threat comes because in another part of our globe there is shadow and darkness ... where many millions suffer under brutal dictatorship, where a third of our planet lives in a poverty beyond anything even the poorest in our societies can imagine, and where a fanatical strain of religious extremism has arisen. . . . And because in the combination of these afflictions a new and deadly virus has emerged. The virus is terrorism, whose intent to inflict destruction is unconstrained by human feeling and whose capacity to inflict it is enlarged by technology."

In the face of such a threat, said Blair, the idea of Europe competing with America as an alternative center of power was "dangerous" and an "anachronism." What was needed was partnership to face the common threats. "If Europe and America are together, the rest will work with us. If we split ... nothing but mischief will be the result." What Blair really feared above all else was America being driven into isolationism.

There were many other governments—Italy, Romania, Bulgaria, Poland, Australia, Spain, are only a few—which feared the same and believed also that the United States was right to take military action at this time against Saddam. The Australian government under John Howard had been constant throughout and its Special Forces had played a significant role during the war. In Europe, Blair could point out that despite the posturing of France, Germany, Belgium, and Luxembourg, most governments supported Washington. Poland's contribution was particularly striking; in September the Poles took command of an entire sector of Iraq. Ukraine had the next largest number of troops; other contributors included Spain, Bulgaria, Denmark, Hungary, Latvia, Romania, and Slovakia. Altogether by September 2003, more than thirty countries (apart from the United States and Britain) had over 16,000 troops on the ground in Iraq.

*

In every sense, the stakes now are immensely high. By the fall of 2003, not even the greatest optimists in the Pentagon were expecting their invasion to rewrite the map of the Middle East entirely (at least not yet). Even so, America's actions were unprecedented and daunting. By promising a more decent order in Baghdad, America hoped to spell the end of the ancien régimes of the area. No wonder that the Alawite minority rulers in Syria, the theocrats in Iran, and the princes in Saudi Arabia reacted nervously, even angrily to regime change in Baghdad. It is the domino effect of a reasonable regime in Iraq that they fear. What did President Hosni Mubarak of Egypt have to gain from Iraq being turned from a prison and a basket case into a thriving society, challenging Egypt's own special relationship with Washington?

Hard questions have to be asked of the region in which most of the current governments fear a successful democratic experiment in their backyard. It may not be comfortable diplomatically or economically, given the West's (and Asia's) dependence on Middle East oil, but the practical and moral question that demands an answer is this: Can we afford to continue to do business with these obsolescent polities that rule through repression? The parallel question, of course, is what is the price of democracy if it might lead to takeovers by Islamic extremists?

It is clear that the United States should not extend its occupation of Iraq beyond the point needed to create a functioning administration that can defend itself. But America's presence is vital for now. To French and other propagandists who complained that the (temporary) loss of Iraqi sovereignty was as an intolerable affliction, Fouad Ajami replied, "The custodians of Arab power, and the vast majority of the Arab political class, never saw or named the terrible cruelties of Saddam. A political culture that averts its gaze from mass graves and works itself into self-righteous hysteria over a foreign presence in an Arab country is a culture that has turned its back on political reason."

Radical Islam poses a mortal threat to the world we have created since 1945. Ayatollah Khomeini expressed the ambition in 1984: "If one allows the infidels to continue playing their role as corrupters on Earth, their eventual mortal punishment will be all the stronger. Thus, if we kill the infidels in order to put a stop to their [corrupting] activities, we have indeed done them a service. For their eventual punishment will be less. War is a blessing for the world and for every nation. It is Allah himself who commands men to wage war and kill." That vision inspires Al Qaeda too.

Volume upon volume has already been written about the reasons for the growth of Islamic consciousness and, also, of Islamic terror. Samuel Huntington, who famously coined the phrase "the clash of civilizations" at the beginning of the 1990s, now argues that the Islamic resurgence is "in large part a response to modernization and globalization."

Huntington points out that twenty-three of the thirty conflicts that were under way around the world at the beginning of the twenty-first century involved Muslims. This is not because of Islam itself but because of the growth of Muslim consciousness. "In addition, throughout the Muslim world, and particularly among Arabs, there exists a great sense of grievance, resentment, envy, and hostility towards the West and particularly the United States."

The closeness of the United States to Israel is one of the most important reasons, but not the only one. A solution to the grim deadlock between Israel and the Palestinians has still to be sought for the sake of both people above all. But such a solution will not assuage Islamic hatred of America.

American success in Iraq may increase the anger of the already enraged. But if the United States can help the Iraqis build a decent society, it will have shown once again to all those who are prepared to see that, aside from protecting its own interests, the United States is still the only country that can really change the world for the better.

Those who discount the nature of the threat should consider not only what Islamic terrorists have already done but also what they promise for the future. Behind the bluster, threats like this from Al Qaeda spokesman Suleiman Abu Gheith display true intent: "We have not reached parity with them. We have the right to kill 4 million Americans— 2 million of them children—and to exile twice as many and wound and cripple hundreds of thousands. Furthermore, it is our right to fight them with chemical and biological weapons, so as to afflict them with the fatal maladies that have afflicted the Muslims because of the [Americans'] chemical and biological weapons."

In September 2003 a "ranking Taliban source" told *Newsweek* that bin Laden's priority "is to use biological weapons." The only question is how to transport and launch them. "Osama's next step will be unbelievable."

This is the language of men who seek to destroy the foundations of the international community that we have created since 1945. It is hardly surprising that Tony Blair told the U.S. Congress that he was utterly convinced of the need to do everything possible to stop terrorism and weapons of mass destruction being joined.

Success in the badly named war on terror is hard to quantify. There has been no major attack on the U.S. mainland since 9/11. Afghanistan is no longer a terrorist sanctuary where Al Qaeda can recruit and train its killers at will. Instead, it has been scattered, its networks dispersed, and many of its fundraising opportunities eroded. But it has not been eliminated. Many senior Al Qaeda leaders are still free, including of course bin Laden himself. Its funding is still strong, and it is more active than ever on the Internet.

To some extent Afghanistan has fallen victim to the shift of attention to Iraq. The world's promise to invest troops and money has been cut back or put on hold. Afghanistan remains insecure and anarchic. Taliban forces are regrouping in remote areas of Pakistan, unrestrained, for whatever reason, by the Pakistani authorities. The United States is doing as badly as ever in its campaign for the hearts and minds of the Arab and Islamic worlds. Probably even progress along the "road map" to peace between Israel and the Palestinians will not affect this.

In an October 2003 memorandum that was leaked, Donald Rumsfeld cited "mixed results" against the leaders of Al Qaeda, "reasonable progress" in tracking down top Saddam officials, and "somewhat slower progress" against the Taliban. The United States, he said, "faced a long, hard slog" in Iraq and Afghanistan.

On October 26 Paul Wolfowitz was almost killed in a rocket attack on the Al Rashid Hotel. The next day, the first of the Muslim holy month of Ramadan, the office of the

International Committee of the Red Cross and several police stations were attacked by suicide bombers in Baghdad. Thirty-four people were killed at once and more than 200 wounded. Kofi Annan called the attack on the Red Cross a "crime against humanity." He was right. Yet again, the bombers showed that they would recognize no moral restraints whatsoever in their determination to destroy America's attempt to give a better life to Iraqis.

This tragic reality was brought home yet again by the attack on an American helicopter on November 2, when fifteen soldiers were killed outright and many more were wounded. Not for nothing did Fouad Ajami write "There is something both noble and heartbreaking about those embattled young soldiers standing sentry in what for them must be an incomprehensible place."

There were many different motives in Washington, London, Madrid, Canberra, and among the other allies who joined the war against Saddam Hussein. One fundamental reason for the war was that after 9/11 the U.S. administration was no longer prepared to tolerate the inevitable threat that Saddam posed. There was another shared ambition: This was a genuinely brave attempt, led by the United States, to change the rules in a game where everyone except the tyrants are the losers.

It is difficult to exaggerate how great the stakes are. This is a war that will determine America's place in the world for many years to come. It will mark either a retreat to isolation, or it will underscore its role as guarantor of the freedoms of other democracies, a role that it assumed not once but repeatedly in the twentieth century.

The twentieth century has rightly been called the American Century. Much of what was bravest and best during that century came from America or was sustained by American support and by the knowledge of American partnership. America, more than any other single nation, has a vested interest in the world it helped create and largely pay for during the past 100 years.

Reconstruction is always difficult. In 1945 the novelist John dos Passos made a tour of Europe on assignment for *Life*. American troops were worried. " 'We've lost the peace,' men tell you. 'We can't make it stick.'... Europeans, friend and foe alike, look you accusingly in the face and tell you how bitterly they are disappointed in you as an American." Liberation no longer meant the end of the Nazis "Now it stands in the minds of the civilians for one thing, looting. Never has American prestige in Europe been lower."

And yet, in the end no occupation and reconstruction was more successful than that of America in postwar Europe. All Europeans have America to thank for the success of the Marshall Plan, and all subsequent U.S. assistance.

America and its partners now have a huge undertaking in Iraq. Nothing like this has ever been tried before in the Middle East. A state that deserves to be called fascist has been removed, above all, by the blood of American boys. The construction of a new government that observes even the fundamental rules of civil society would have the power to transform the area.

Kanan Makiya, the Iraqi historian and former exile, says that the United States "has given the people of Iraq a gift—in part for its own national security reasons, selfish reasons, which is perfectly natural. It is up to us to make something of that gift, and make it work. We need your help."

Similarly, Maysoon Al-Damluji, a founding member of the Iraqi Independent Democrats and president of the Independent Iraqi Women's Group, who has returned to Baghdad, spoke of hope. "The Americans rid the Iraqis of Saddam Hussein. Although Iraq will have to go through a long period of finding and understanding itself, the Americans have given us the hope and the opportunity to do so."

Al-Damluji pointed out that, apart from security, two of the most important problems for Iraq were dealing with Saddam's massive debts, around $150 billion, and negotiating with Turkey over dams on the Tigris and the Euphrates. Already, American legal experts were aiding Iraqi lawyers on both matters.

"What Iraqis need most of all today is to open up at last

to the rest of the world. The Americans are helping us do this through exchange programmes on academic, professional and civil society levels. They are also developing education, promoting human rights studies, and modern sciences. They are encouraging Iraqis to form civic societies such as women's groups, professional groups, NGOs and political parties."

I quoted at the beginning of this short book the UN Development Programme report on Arab society. Written by Arabs themselves, it showed that one reason for the Arab world falling so far behind the rest is because of the corrupt, autocratic, and reactionary nature of the prevailing political systems built on nationalism, socialism, and brutality. The new Iraq offers an opportunity to discard that model in favor of something better. The coalition led by America has given hope to Iraqis.

Kanan Makiya points out, "We're talking about beginning something in Iraq which eventually changes the perception of the United States in that part of the world. . . . We are not talking about military adventures all over the world . . . one after another. No sensible person should be talking that way. We're talking about an alternative to the autocracies." The war in Iraq is not just about WMD. It is about the relationship of the United States to an area of vital concern and immense importance that has become politically degraded in recent decades.

If, having embarked upon this risky course, American resolve fails and it is compelled by the Saddamites and the Islamist suicide bombers to withdraw, the consequences would be incalculable. It would be a disaster not merely to the millions of Iraqis, finally daring to hope that the curse of Saddam is gone forever. Unless America and its allies prevail, Iraq will become a vast playground for terrorist activity, a far more dangerous haven than Afghanistan used to be.

If America and its allies cannot fight this new war, dictators and zealots everywhere will rejoice at how easily the United States can be deterred, and all those countries that look to America to defend their stability and security will lose faith. Just as it would have been a Cold War catastrophe if the United States had backed down during the 1962 Cuban Missile Crisis, it would be similarly catastrophic to abandon Iraq now. Not only for Iraq itself, but also for America and the world. The battle in Iraq is between those who have committed mass murder or wish to, and those who seek a decent civil society. It is the most important battle of our time.

The arguments about preemption will continue—and they should. But even this most contentious doctrine is not at the heart of the crisis that has tested the Western democratic allies. Tony Blair and George W. Bush and their partners in countries as far afield as Australia, Italy, Poland, and Spain, were courageous in their determination finally to confront a regime that was an intolerable burden to its own people and an unacceptable affront to the world. They understood that the marriage—of new technology and new terrorism—brings threats that have to be met before they are carried out.

I repeat, America and the West have made serious mistakes in Iraq. Intelligence was wrong—Saddam's WMD ambitions were an inevitable threat rather than an immediate one. The U.S. was woefully unprepared for the postwar administration of the country and was surprised by the extent of the guerrilla war that it would have to fight. Iraqis were not properly engaged early enough. Vital time was lost. The United Nations system could at times have been used more skillfully. Those of us like myself who supported the invasion must lament all these mistakes and their consequences.

As this book went to press the security crisis in Iraq was growing. That was happening precisely because most Iraqis' lives were improving. The enemies of America and of a better Iraq were ferociously trying to kill all progress.

The relentless growth in murderous attacks upon the

coalition forces and upon Iraqis who yearned to improve their country was horrifying and heartbreaking.

Hatred of America is a powerful and a very destructive force in the world today. Some of that hatred is caused by America's mistakes, though that is not true of the rage of Islamic nihilists, a minority that nothing can assuage. I believe the bottom line is this: For all its faults, American commitment and American sacrifice are essential to the world. As in the twentieth century, so in the twenty-first, only America has both the power and the optimism to defend the international community against what really are forces of darkness.

Nothing like the struggle for Iraq has been tried before in the Middle East. Tony Blair argues with consistent courage that the overthrow of the outlaw Saddam regime and the promise to build a decent state was "the right thing to do." He is correct but we are seeing how immensely difficult the task now is.

The responsibility on America and its allies is immense. The only certainty is that they must succeed. The alternatives are too terrible to contemplate.

Chapter 7

"DEMOCRACY IS COMING AND THERE WILL BE NO EXCUSE THEREAFTER"

E LECTIONS really do matter—especially to people who have been denied them. In the UN-managed elections of 1993, millions of Cambodians braved threats from the Khmer Rouge to vote in the only free elections they had ever been granted. (The UN was then unable to guarantee the result for which the people had voted.) In Algeria in 1995, when the government—almost overcome by years of Islamic terrorist assault—called elections, the much-abused majority defied the terrorist threats and voted en masse. In Afghanistan, the people confounded the Western critics and scoffers and, despite Taliban threats, voted overwhelmingly to try to put the curse of Islamic extremism behind them. Afghan women, until recently utterly suppressed by the Taliban, led the lines to many polling stations.

And on January 30, 2005, we saw it most brutally and most clearly in Iraq, when the Iraqi people voted in the freest elections they—or any other Arabs—had ever experienced.

Until the very morning of the vote, many commentators had predicted that the constant threat of terrorist attack upon voters and the polling stations would stop the vast majority of electors going to the polls. This war against the Iraqi people was being waged by the same people, Sunni Baathists, who had oppressed them for decades and wished to do so again, ably abetted by the Islamo-fascist Sunni jihadists led by Osama bin Laden's Heydrich in Iraq, the Jordanian terrorist Abu Musab al-Zarqawi.

At one level the elections were a theocratic struggle between Sunni and Shia; the struggle against Al Qaeda and the Baathists was led by the Ayatollah al-Sistani, the principal leader of the Shiites, who make up over 60 percent of the Iraqi population. Al-Sistani, who had since April 2003 embraced a policy of cautious co-operation with the American-led occupation, told his followers that it was their duty to vote. By contrast, in a video aired on Al Jazeera, bin Laden declared that, "Anyone who participates in these elections...has committed apostasy against Allah." He endorsed killing of security people in the new government—"their blood is permitted. They are apostates whose deaths should not be prayed over."

Al-Zarqawi described the Shia as "the lurking snakes and the crafty scorpions, the spying enemy and the penetrating venom, the most evil of mankind." Every day he murdered more. In late January a car bomber killed fourteen people, including children, as they left their mosque in Baghdad.

Most visibly, he murdered Ayatollah Baqir al-Hakim, the head of SCIRI, one of the principal Shiite parties, and later tried to murder his brother and successor. In that attack thirteen other Iraqis were killed and sixty-six wounded.

More powerful were the Baathists who wished to restore a Saddamite dictatorship. Several Sunni military leaders had been arrested in the successful American assault upon their stronghold, Fallujah, in November 2004. One was Colonel Muayed al-Nasseri, who recounted that Saddam had set up his group, Mohammed's Army, after the fall of Baghdad. Under interrogation by the U.S. military, he said that they had been receiving aid from both Iran and Syria, neither of which wish to see a democracy in Iraq. He said Iran had given them "one million dollars. . . cars, weapons. . . even car bombs."

The impact of the terrorist insurgency was huge and for a time it looked as if the elections might have to be delayed. Many of the political parties did not dare name their candidates, for fear they would be murdered. Public meetings were virtually impossible. Terrorist groups warned that polling stations would be bombed indiscriminately on election day.

But dogged arrangements continued nonetheless. One of the foreign heroes of the process was Carlos Valenzuela, a Columbian who was the chief UN election official in Baghdad. In the weeks leading up to the poll, he was asked constantly if legitimate elections could take place despite the non-stop wholesale murders. He replied Yes. "Look," he said, "in my country we have elections that are not perfect, that have been marred by violence and terrible intimidation. But still people go to the polls. And still the results are accepted as legitimate."

If one image epitomized the seriousness of what was at stake in this election, it was the photograph in mid-December of three election officials being dragged from their car in Baghdad and murdered, on camera, in the street. As Tony Blair said in Baghdad that same month, "On the one side you have people who desperately want to make the democratic process work, and want to have the same type of democratic freedoms other parts of the world enjoy, and on the other side people who are killing and intimidating and trying to destroy a better future for Iraq. Our response should be to stand alongside the democrats."

Although the bombings and shootings increased in the weeks leading up to the poll, the Iraqi people still seemed determined to vote for a new Iraq. A survey conducted in Iraq in January by the London paper, *Al-Sharq Al-Awsat*, found that 66 percent of those questioned wanted the elections to go ahead on schedule. Iraqi women, who constitute a clear majority of Iraqi population, were particularly interested. According to another survey by Women for Women International in Baghdad, Mosul, and Basra, "94 percent of women surveyed want to secure legal rights for women; 84 percent of women wanted the right to vote on the final constitution; [and] nearly 80 percent of women believe that their participation in local and national councils should not be limited." The report noted, "the most unexpected result of the survey is that despite increasing violence, particularly violence against women, 90.6 percent of Iraqi women reported that they are hopeful about their future." Iraqis, like Cambodians, Algerians, and the Afghans, clearly wished to defy those who sought to murder, mutilate, and incarcerate them.

Nonetheless, such was the violence that even the interim Prime Minister, Ayad Allawi, suggested to Washington that delay might be necessary. President Bush refused to consider it.

On election day, the security cordons drawn by the coalition and Iraqi forces around the towns and the polling stations were tighter then ever. The new Iraqi security forces acquitted themselves much better than many people had expected. Terrorist attacks killed thirty-five people, but 60 percent of voters throughout the country managed to vote. In many places, as had happened in Afghanistan, it was the women who were bravest and went first to the polls, returning home to show their men that they had gone, voted, had their fingers stained, and were safely home. Men followed. When they returned home, whole families and communities held their stained fingers aloft in joy and triumph.

Every voter was able to cast two votes, one for the national assembly and another for one of the eighteen provincial councils. Voters in Kurdistan also elected an autonomous Kurdish parliament.

Overall, 7471 candidates on eleven different lists competed for 275 seats in the National Assembly. Almost 8,000 more candidates stood for seats on the provincial councils. Altogether, an average of fourteen candidates ran for each seat, high by western standards but perhaps a demonstration of the thirst for political representation after so many decades of denial.

In the end about 8.45 million voters cast their ballots. When they were counted, the Shiite coalition, the Iraqi National Alliance, emerged with the largest number of seats, as expected. But it did not have an absolute majority.

The Kurds (who make up around 20 percent of the population) won 27 percent of the vote. The most troubling aspect of the poll was that, under pressure from their leaders and for fear of the Sunni terrorists, most Sunnis boycotted the election. As a result they had only seventeen members of the new assembly.

The losers were the current leadership. Ayad Allawi, a secular Shia, had been robust in the face of the insurrection, but he was blamed by voters for failing to defeat it, and for continuing shortages in such basic amenities as drinking water, electricity, gasoline, and gas for home cooking. In one sense Allawi's failure could be called a success— it is not often that Arab governments lose an election.

Almost one third of the new parliamentarians were women—more than almost anywhere else in the world and an extraordinary event in an Arab country, and one with huge repercussions for the future of the Islamic world. The new representatives found agreement difficult, but before the second anniversary of Saddam's overthrow on April 9, 2005, they had selected a new leadership. When one remembers that Iraq had hitherto been run by a dictatorship of the tiny Sunni minority, its composition was remarkable. The President was the longtime Kurdish leader and enemy of Saddam Hussein, Jalal Talabani. The new Prime Minister was to be a Shia, Ibrahim al-Ja'afari, who had had long links with Teheran. In other words, under American guidance, the despised and persecuted peoples of Iraq were now in control.

This was all revolutionary enough. But the election was only the first stage of reform. The National Assembly now had to draw up a new constitution, to be adopted by August 15, 2005. This was be presented to a referendum by October 15, 2005, and a new election was to be held under the new constitution for a permanent national assembly by December 15, 2005. It was all a formidable challenge and the enemies of progress were by no means defeated. Indeed, after a post-election lull, the violence against the new state became as bloody as ever.

It is important to note that in the two years since the overthrow of Saddam, many milestones which had once been judged unreachable have been passed. It is self-evident that nothing has given the Iraqi people a greater sense of self confidence than their courage in voting in such large numbers in January 2005. Despite the horrific, violent counter-attacks, the country is being transformed. And its transformation is having an enormous impact upon the region.

Almost a year earlier, in mid-March 2004, I traveled in Iraq with Emma Bonino, an Italian politician and friend. Every

Iraqi we met confirmed the findings of the extensive poll, conducted by the Oxford Research Centre and published by the BBC and other broadcasters that March. The majority of Iraqis said that their lives were better now than before the invasion and 70 percent said they felt that their lives would be better still in a year's time—one third saying, Much Better. About half said they opposed the presence of coalition forces but few wanted them to leave immediately.

In Nasariyah, one of the poorest provinces, security had worsened recently, with both gangs of criminals and fundamentalist militias marauding. We met Sabri al-Rumadia, the newly-nominated Governor of Nasariyah. He was proud that the marshes, which Saddam had drained in a brutal act of ethnic cleansing, were being refilled. The Marsh Arabs were returning, though they would never be able to come back in such numbers as before.

He said that the priorities were economy, transport, and security. The lack of security—though not everywhere—was one of the greatest failures of the Coalition and understandably one of the principal reasons for growing disillusion with the occupation.

Bonino asked him, "What is your message to the world?"

He replied, "It is to say : 'Please send any help you can to Iraq. Don't stay away. That would be a big disaster for us.'"

He was horrified by what had happened in Spain. A few days after the Al Qaeda bombings in Madrid, the electorate had voted out of power the conservative government led by Jose Maria Aznar, one of the staunchest supporters of the war in Iraq. The socialist victors had decreed a swift withdrawal from the Coalition.

The governor thought such withdrawal was very harmful to the hopes of a new Iraq. "It is essential that the coalition forces stay to put pressure on our neighbours (especially Iran) not to interfere." Iranian subversive and terrorist interference, said he and others, was very serious.

We met with some ten women, representing themselves or other groups, like teachers. Emma Bonino asked, "Do you think life has changed a bit for the better or not?" One of them answered, "We have great hope for the future. The problem is now."

After Nasariyah, we flew to Baghdad. The city seemed surreal. The first impression driving off Saddam's vast military airfield and into the city was of the dictator's insane megalomania, as Saddam's palaces rolled by. We went first to the Coalition Provisional Authority (CPA) headquarters, heavily protected by concrete walls, in the old Royal Palace, which had been expanded by Saddam. At the heavily-fortified entrance, a GI said through the car window, "Smile, guys, you're in Baghdad." Inside the Palace, there were (rather pleasingly) GI cots under Saddam's murals of ICBMs. There we saw Paul Bremer, the head of the CPA. He argued that, "The most important fact of life here now is that the Iraqis are free and are embracing democracy." Debate and argument were everywhere. The U.S. was committed to spend $1/2 billion on democracy-building programs. $27 million of this was to be used to set up women's centers and teach women's rights in every province.

The impact of the mistakes made by the Coalition was also clear. As Gwyn Prins, the legal and military scholar, put it, these included "decisions not to deploy a reserve Division, not to deploy [or maybe even to possess] a detailed political strategy for the critical days immediately after Saddam's statue was toppled, and hence not to have issued rules of engagement or tasks to troops in Baghdad to prevent looting and to secure the allegiance of the Baathist civil servants. In the same vein was the decision to disband the Iraqi army and police." Prins argued that many U.S. mistakes flowed from a reluctance to recognize that it is now an imperial actor, that Washington cannot persist "in the illusion that its job is to liberate and then to depart. . . . In the face of the twenty-first century, America has no choice about whether to be an imperial power or not; that is prescribed by circumstance. The choice is between doing the job competently or incompetently."

Outside the Green Zone, behind the headlines of the awful violence of car bombers and other terrorist attacks, there was another reality. Unemployment was certainly very serious. The U.S.'s $18 billion aid program was late—much too late—in delivery. There was no good explanation for the slowness of reconstruction in the year gone by. But Baghdad was a boom city. Every corner was piled high with boxes of air conditioners, televisions, and other consumer durables for sale. There was an explosion of ideas as well as consumer goods. The interim constitution, adopted by the Governing Council in March, gave citizens, and particularly women, more rights than they had ever enjoyed in any neighboring states. It was truly a revolutionary document. The question that women, in particular, asked, was "Will it last?"

Children were back at school in most of Iraq—and they no longer just had to worship Saddam. Almost all hospitals were re-opened. There had already been municipal elections in seventeen Iraqi cities, and in each of them victory had gone to democratic and secularist parties—similarly in professional associations. All the opinion polls favored democratization.

Fifteen months earlier there were only pro-Saddam newspapers and television. Now there were over 200 newspapers and satellite dishes, outlawed under Saddam, that were wildly popular. The two principal Arabic broadcasters, Al Jazeera and Al Arabiya, although opposed to the American-led venture in Iraq, owed their popularity to the fact that the new dispensation allowed Iraqis to hear their news and views. Al Jazeera, in particular, broadcast poison. But debate on the streets flourished as result.

We met with a group of young people—students and artists amongst them. "The end of Saddam was like a dream," said one. "Now we can talk for the first time in our lives." "The Coalition has not protected our security well enough," said another. A third said, "We believe Saddam himself was the real Weapon of Mass Destruction. We have freedom now... Don't leave now."

By the time Bonino and I concluded our short visit, it was impossible not to be infected by the optimism and to believe the polls showing that most Iraqis were glad that the Coalition had overthrown Saddam, and they were, for the first time, enjoying many of the freedoms taken for granted in the West. The sense of relief that Saddam's secret police were no longer listening everywhere was palpable, despite the increasing terrorist assault. It was quite wrong for the new socialist Spanish Prime Minister, Jose Luis Rodriguez Zapatero, to describe Iraq as "a disaster." On the contrary, the disaster would be to turn away from the commitment we had given the Iraqi people and ourselves.

Soon after I left Baghdad, the terrorist assault upon the new Iraq grew in intensity and horror—perhaps because of the successful adoption of the Transitional Administrative Law, which guaranteed pluralistic, open government and protected minorities—it was the antithesis of despotism and rigid Islamic sharia law.

In January 2004, the coalition forces intercepted a letter from al-Zarqawi. He told his colleagues that "democracy" in Iraq would bring "suffocation" to their cause, as would the prospect of Iraqis fighting in their own defense. Once the army and police were "linked to the inhabitants of this area by kinship, blood and honour," he asked, "how can we fight their cousins and their sons and under what pretext after the Americans pull back? . . . Democracy is coming and there will be no excuse thereafter." The choice, he wrote, was war, or "packing our bags and looking for a new field of battle, as has been the case in other campaigns of jihad, because our enemy grows stronger with every passing day."

The brutal, indiscriminate attacks upon Iraqis and members of the coalition in the first eight months of 2004 were designed to weaken the jihadists' enemy, in every way possible. When the Americans practiced more sophisticated force protection and their own troops became harder to attack, the terrorists turned to softer targets—the smaller partners in the Coalition, like Italy, Western contractors, and Iraqi officials of the new administration. This threat to Iraqis lost the terrorists a lot of sympathy amongst the population, but it also caused rising popular fury at the occupiers' inability to protect the people. The task for the occupiers was to ensure that the vast majority of the Iraqi people remained convinced that the whole purpose of the invasion—providing them with a country ruled with the consent of its people—could be realized.

At the end of March 2004, Iraqi insurgents in the Sunni town of Fallujah, north of Baghdad, which had become a center of resistance to the Coalition, seized four American civilian contractors, butchered them, danced around their corpses, dismembered them, and hung their body parts on a bridge. It was a gruesome assault which had deliberate echoes of the attack on American soldiers in Somalia in 1993 that had led to President Clinton withdrawing all U.S. forces from the country, which in turn led Osama bin laden to declare that America was only "a weak horse" which could easily be beaten.

The response to Falluja was initially different: the Bush

administration insisted that the murderers of the contractors must be punished. In April, the U.S. Marines were sent
to Fallujah to try and deal with the terrorists, who took
refuge in mosques from which they fired upon the Marines.
Robert Kaplan, an experienced correspondent embedded
with the Marines, was able to show that they went to great
length to avoid damaging mosques and civilians. Nonetheless the coverage of the siege in the Arab media, and in
much of the Western press, was hostile.

The pervasive Arab satellite channels began to talk of
the "Fallujah butchery" and to present Fallujah as "one of
the greatest battles the Arabs have ever waged against the
Crusaders." Arab poets wrote poems commemorating Fallujah as "the Arab Stalingrad"; a Syrian composer com-
menced an opera about the "heroes of Fallujah."

It was pernicious nonsense. The Red Crescent society of
the United Arab Emirates, which had a hospital in Fallujah,
reported that, "The fighting concerned only a few districts
of the town. There was never any fighting on a big scale.
There certainly was no clash involving thousands of the
town's inhabitants. The number of those who died did not
exceed 270, almost all fighters, not civilians. The resistance
[i.e. insurgency] was made up of former Iraqi army officers
with a small number of [non-Iraqi] Arabs repressing [radi-
cal Islamist] groups."

But the anti-American propaganda was so strong that members of the Governing Council, America's allies, felt the need to denounce the operation. Shia from the south of Iraq declared that they would form an alliance with their traditional Sunni enemies in the besieged town. Even Lakhdar Brahimi, the UN special envoy in Iraq, attacked the Marines' conduct in the town as "collective punishment" of the population.

Washington should have countered such polemics. But, as so often in the case of Iraq, American public diplomacy was woefully inadequate. As Robert Kaplan wrote, "The Bush administration should have been holding dramatic public slide shows for the public. . . explaining how this or that particular mosque was being militarily utilized, and how much was being done to avoid destroying them, at great risk to Marine lives."

Kaplan pointed out that there were many different realities in Iraq, and in the modern war of perceptions, victory is too easily awarded to those with the most compelling narrative. "Truly, in the world of post-modern twenty-first-century conflict, civilian and military public affairs officers must become war fighters by another name. They must control and anticipate a whole new storm system represented by a global media, which too often exposes embarrassing facts out of historical or philosophical context." The Bush administration's failure in this regard has been very clear. There is, amongst the bad news in which Iraq's enemies rejoice and which they exploit, much good news from Iraq.

Instead, in the face of the successful propaganda, the Bush administration decided that the political cost of destroying the terrorist safe area that it had [correctly] identified as a threat to the new Iraq was too high. Given the choice of appearing ruthless or "a weak horse," it chose the latter. It even decided to use the services of a Baathist general, once close to Saddam, to try and effect some policing of the town.

This may have placated some Western commentators. It did not give confidence to many Iraqis. One senior British officer in Iraq wrote that while "the West breathed a sigh of [sanctimonious] relief. . . the near-universal Iraqi reaction was to brand the Coalition as weak." A spokesman for Ayatollah al-Sistani, the de facto leader of the Shiite majority in Iraq, warned that "members of the Baath party committed the most heinous crimes and created bloodbaths and the biggest mass graves in the history of mankind."

U.S. military officials also knew that by deciding to allow such people to control Fallujah, the Coalition was in effect creating a safe area for terrorists and insurgents there. Through most of 2004, groups controlled by Saddamite officers and by al-Zarqawi used the city as a place to assemble car bombs, which they then dispatched along with their

killer suicide drivers to Baghdad and other cities. Iraqi officials told *The New York Times* that former members of the
Baath party held a conference there in early summer 2004
to plot their return to power. By the time of the hand-over
of sovereignty to Iraq at the end of June, U.S. officers
openly acknowledged that force would have to be used
against them in the end. At the end of 2004, the U.S.
Marines finally laid siege to the city to destroy it as a safe
haven for the terrorists. They discovered dozens of prisons
and torture chambers in which scores if not hundreds of
hostages had been imprisoned, tortured, and murdered.

The U.S.-led campaign to rebuild Iraq endured many setbacks, some of them self-inflicted. Few were more serious
than the revelation at the end of April 2004 that some
American guards had been abusing Iraqi prisoners in Abu
Ghraib prison in Baghdad. This had a disastrous impact;
the photographs of sexual and other humiliations that
were instantly broadcast around the world inevitably
diminished the strength of America's moral cause in the
eyes of many beholders. But there was no way in which the
abuses carried out by some American troops, appalling
though they were, could properly be compared to the systematic torture the Saddam regime had inflicted upon its

victims. Indeed, the new Iraqi minister for Human Rights criticized the abuses at Abu Ghraib but asked where the Arab protest had been during the long Saddam years when Iraqis were being tortured to death.

The difference was also shown in the response to the abuses. Saddam murdered and tortured hundreds of thousands of people—millions, indeed, over decades and with impunity. By contrast, long before the photographs from Abu Ghraib became public, the U.S. military authorities had begun investigations into the abuses; they quickly identified the culprits and initiated judicial proceedings against them. The report of the investigating officer, Major-General Antonio Taguba, was conscientious and recounted that "numerous incidents of sadistic, blatant and wanton criminal abuses were inflicted on several detainees." His report gave specific details of the crimes of military police personnel. By the time the infamous photographs reached the public domain, criminal charges had already been brought against six of the soldiers involved. The independent inquiry headed by former Defense Secretary James Schlesinger concluded in summer 2004 that despite allegations, the Abu Ghraib abuses were not linked to interrogations. No evidence was ever produced to show that the abuses were "systematic" or condoned, let alone inspired by senior officers or officials.

In May 2004, Sabrina Harman, an Army reservist who appeared in several of the abuse photographs, was sentenced to six months in prison for her role in the scandal. Two Iraqi prisoners at Abu Ghraib, whose testimony was read into the record, said the former pizza shop manager had treated them very well at Abu Ghraib. "She has no cruelty in her," said Amjad Ismail Khalil al-Taie through an interpreter. "Even though she is an American woman, she was just like a sister."

Harman, however, accepted responsibility. She wept and apologized for the mistreatment she had helped inflict. "As a soldier and military police officer, I failed my duties and failed my mission to protect and defend," Harman said. "I not only let down the people in Iraq, but I let down every single soldier that serves today." Acknowledging that her conduct had increased hatred for the United States, she said, "I take full responsibility for my actions. . . . The decisions I made were mine and mine alone."

The French philosopher Andre Glucksman argued that, far from undermining the basic moral authority of the United States, the Abu Ghraib scandal actually reinforced the fact that it was the world's "most exemplary" democracy, ". . . the only one where Congressional committees summon a president, secretaries, generals, [and] heads of secret services and interrogate them unabashed and with-

out restrictions. Let me remind here that France, so gener-
ous at giving lessons, has not in forty years indicted, judged,
or condemned a single one of the soldiers who committed
torture during the Algeria war."

The difference between the inexcusable abuse of prisoners by some American troops and the torture systemati-
cally inflicted during the Saddam years was explicit in
videos made during the Saddam era in which prisoners
were shown having their hands chopped off, arms broken,
and tongues torn out. According to Nick Schulz, an American documentary producer who has seen these videos, they
are almost impossible to watch.

> One clip opens amid Saddam's elite troops, Saddam Feday-
> een, chanting 'With blood and spirit we will redeem you
> Saddam.' The Fedayeen stand barking and clapping in a
> courtyard. A blindfolded prisoner, forced to his knees and
> held in position has his arm outstretched before him along
> a low concrete wall. A masked member of the Fedayeen
> raises high a three-foot-long blade and ferociously slams
> down on the man's hand, slicing through his finger tips.
> The victim is wailing, screaming in agony. The swordsman-
> torturer, not sufficiently satisfied with his first effort, raises
> the sword again and drives down once more on the man's
> immobile hand. This time he severs the fingers closer to

the knuckles as the blood spurts from [the prisoner's] hand, spilling over and down the concrete slab. The victim emits a wail I have never heard—could never imagine hearing—from a grown main, this time louder, harder than the first. The camera then turns to the assembled Fedayeen as they continue rhythmically chanting....

In another clip, a hooded and blindfolded prisoner is led to a room where he is forced to kneel, hands tied behind his back. Another man sits before the prisoner with thick metal tweezers and a scalpel. With his left hand he grabs the prisoner's tongue with the tweezers and pulls it forward from his head. With the scalpel in his other hand, he slices through the prisoner's tongue, cutting it from his mouth and then dropping it on the floor. This ritual is repeated for more prisoners who are lined up, squatting in a row like parts on an assembly line....

I was unable to sit through these clips at first, having to turn away several times.... These film clips reveal—and help one 'appreciate'—the fullness of the inhuman, soulless horror of Saddam's regime. They reveal the character and moral constitution of the foe Coalition forces must reckon with on a daily basis.

But it was the pictures of the limited American abuses in Abu Ghraib that dominated the news, not the wholesale horrors of the Saddam era. From then on, Abu Ghraib was invoked by the enemies of Saddam's overthrow to try and call into question the entire basis of "Operation Iraqi Freedom."

As the terrorist attacks in Iraq increased and opposition to the Coalition was expressed across the Islamic world, Washington's critics argued that the overthrow of Saddam had also been a serious error because it was inflaming Islamic extremism. Bin Laden himself said as much.

Well, that is an important factor. But is it and should it be the most important? The first Gulf war, fought to liberate Kuwait, provoked one of bin Laden's early clarion calls for holy war. Should we therefore have left Kuwait in the hands of Saddam? No. For similar reasons, the opportunistic rage of bin Laden to the overthrow of Saddam was not a reason to desist.

The hideously painful stand-off between Israel and the Palestinians has been used to create Islamic militants. But even if the destination on the Road Map, a two-state solution for Israel and Palestine, were reached immediately, that would not end the threat from bin Laden and those who think like him. They see this as an existential war. Their ambition is to impose worldwide Islamic theocracy;

their game plan is to use every country as a staging post for the next.

It is not true that Western policy has provoked, let alone created, bin Ladenism. During the 1990s, when there was no war in Iraq, thousands, perhaps tens of thousands of Islamic warriors were trained in the bin Laden camps in Afghanistan. It was a time when the U.S. president, Bill Clinton, was working diligently to create an agreement between Israel and the Palestinians. The United States finally came to the rescue of Muslims in Bosnia, after Europe had failed to do so, and then led the effort to save Muslims in Kosovo.

None of these efforts stopped bin Laden from building up his organization and attacking the U.S. wherever he could. In their book, *The Age of Sacred Terror,* Daniel Benjamin and Steven Simon, senior counterterrorist officials in the Clinton administration, spoke of "tens of thousands" of Islamic fighters being trained in Al Qaeda camps in the '90s.

Osama bin Laden does not himself direct all the terrorist attacks in the western and Arab world. But his doctrine and his extraordinary success in 9/11 have given a new strength and a perverse vision to disparate Islamic groups around the world. They live to kill. The most determined live to die. Or, perhaps more often, they brainwash others to do so.

Kaywan Qader is an 18-year-old Kurd from Suleimaniya,

who was arrested by the Kurdish authorities; this account was published in early 2004 in the London-based Arabic paper *Al-Sharq Al-Awsat*.

> Kaywan Qader was one of ten children in a moderately religious family. In the mosque he met Sawara Ali, who discussed religion with him and then recruited him to [the terrorist group] Ansar al-Islam... He was able to convince Qader that Jihad would offer him paradise and save him from hell. Qader agreed to join Ali in one of the camps to prepare himself for Jihad, and all of his father's efforts to dissuade him from that failed. Qader told his father that Allah's wish supersedes his family's wish.... In the camp Qader agreed to carry out a suicide mission because he was told it is the highest level of jihad......Another detainee who spent time in the camp says that they listened to lectures where they were told that each of the martyrs will find 72 virgins waiting for him in paradise...

Throughout the Islamic world are many others, more sophisticated than Qader, who are keen to take the suicide-murder route.

Alan Dershowitz recounted the example of Majid al-Enezi, a Saudi student training to be a computer technician, who decided to go to Iraq to become a suicide bomber. His brother Abdullah was overjoyed and said that,

"People are calling all the time to congratulate us, crying from happiness and envy." Such people were not driven to their actions by poverty and despair any more than the middle-class 9/11 bombers had been. They were incited by their religious leaders to "kill the infidels" and to believe that suicide bombings were the highest form of jihad. That incitement, reiterated constantly in Arabic press and television, is at the root of such terrorism. To pretend otherwise is a hypocrisy and a delusion.

In Iraq, al-Zarqawi was reported to have been the executioner of the young American, Nicholas Berg, in May 2004. His group also murdered an Italian, Fabrizio Quattrochi, who died with a display of great courage. In June 2004, Saudi terrorists beheaded another American, Paul Johnson, and declared "the infidel got his fair treatment . . ." In July, terrorists in Iraq murdered a South Korean, Kim Sin Il, and a Bulgarian hostage, believed to be Georgi Lazov. They then captured and threatened to murder a Filipino unless the Filipino government immediately withdrew its small humanitarian contingent from Iraq. The Filipino government bowed to this blackmail, an act of national appeasement which will have further resonance within the Philippines, facing its own Islamic rebellion, and beyond. In September 2004, terrorists captured and murdered two Americans, Eugene Armstrong and Jack Hensley, and a British businessman, Ken Begley. Perhaps most stunning of all in its barbarity was the kidnapping and assumed murder of Margaret Hassan, a British woman who had lived for thirty years in Iraq, and had dual British and Iraqi nationality. Her husband was an Iraqi, she loved the country, she was the country director of Care International and she was very much opposed to the U.S.-led invasion. Nonetheless she was targeted. After her abduction, a video film of her begging for her life was distributed; her body was not found. Such murders have continued ever since.

The videos made by the killers have been distributed across the Arab world and North Africa as recruitment tools. They are also intended to terrorize, if not coalition soldiers, at least the foreign civilian workers who are essential to the construction of the new state. Thus a group of Nepalese cooks were captured and murdered. It is hard to imagine anyone more innocent.

The threat was spelled out by an Al Qaeda operative in Saudi Arabia: "We renew our determination to repel the crusader forces and their arrogance, to liberate the land of the Muslims, to apply sharia law and cleanse the Arabian peninsula of infidels."

In this context it is worth noting the words of Fawwaz bin Muhammed Al-Nashami, who commanded the Al Qaeda unit that killed twenty-two people at Khobar, Saudia Arabia, on May 29, 2004.

> We tied the infidel [a Briton] by one leg [behind the car]. . . Everyone watched the infidel being dragged. . . The infidel's clothing was torn to shreds and he was naked in the street. . . praise and gratitude to Allah. . . . We found a Swedish infidel. Brother Nimr cut off his head, and put it on the gate so that it would be seen by all those entering and exiting. . . . We found Filipino Christians. We cut their throats and dedicated them to our brothers the Mujahideen in the Philippines. [Likewise] we found Hindu engineers and we cut their throats too, Allah be praised. . . . Afterwards we turned to the hotel. We entered and found a restaurant, where we ate breakfast and rested a while. Then we went up to the next floor, found several Hindu dogs and cut their throats.

Such hideous orgies are not about Palestine, Abu Ghraib, or even about American actions in Afghanistan or Iraq—though all these are grievances. Instead, they are part of an apocalyptic war to restore the Muslim caliphate and to purge the world of all else but a vile and violent version of Islam. Following the murder of Paul Johnson, the Iranian-French expert, Amir Taheri, wrote, "Paul Johnson was killed by lies spread by Arab elites. He was killed by the sheikhs who finance Arab television and by the anchormen and women who, with tones of false emotion in their voices, told all those lies about Fallujah, just as they have been telling lies about other conflicts involving the Arabs for decades. He was killed by the over 1,500 Arab lawyers who have volunteered to defend Saddam Hussein but were nowhere to be seen when he was engaged in genocide against the Iraqi people. To say that killing Johnson was wrong would mean accepting that he, though not a Muslim, was a full human being with an equal right to live. And that is the huge, historic, indeed doctrinal, leap that Islam must take before it can contain and defeat the terrorists who are trying to change it beyond recognition."

The reality is that Islam is at present engaged in a civil war. One faction—of which Osama bin Laden claims leadership—is totalitarian and preaches the culture of death. That faction glories in 9/11, in the train massacres in Madrid, and in the butchery of the Dutch film maker, Theo van Gogh, for his temerity in making a film critical of the abuse of women under Islam. That faction, responsible also for many of the horrific murders in Iraq, has to be rejected and defeated—above all by moderate Muslims themselves. But it is not a war from which the West can stand aside.

I returned to Iraq in September 2004, exactly three years after 9/11. By now Paul Bremer had left and the Coalition

Provisional Authority had been disbanded. In its place, the Iraqi interim government, under Prime Minister Ayad Allawi, had been created.

Saddam Hussein had made a stunning appearance—the first since he was captured in December 2003. He was brought in chains before an Iraqi court to be told of the crimes against humanity with which he was to be charged.

These included killing members of political parties in the last 30 years; killing religious leaders in 1974; gassing the Kurds in Halabja in 1988; the invasion of Kuwait; and the mass killings during the 1991 uprising against his rule.

In his first brief appearance in the dock, Saddam was not hooded. He had not had his hand chopped off. He was treated in a proper, civilized manner. He was defiant and contemptuous. He insisted that he was still "President of Iraq" and the Kuwaitis he called "dogs." Of the gassing of the Kurds at Halabja, he said, "I heard about that on television." He showed contempt for the process, declaring that, "This is all theatre—the real criminal is Bush." The young judge presiding in the court replied to the man in the dock that in fact his trial was about restoring rights and accountability. It was about the future of Iraq. And on the successful development of civil Iraq, much, much, more depended.

I traveled first to the southern Iraqi town of Basra where the 8,000-strong British army contingent had its headquarters. Basra used to be one of the great trading cities of the Gulf. Now, after thirty years of Saddam's misrule, it was a pitiful, poor slum. Still, since the invasion, economic activity had picked up here as everywhere else in Iraq. Merchants of washing machines, air conditioners, and satellite dishes were doing a roaring trade. Parked on one street was a white stretch limo which some enterprising driver had imported from the Gulf and now hired out for weddings.

But first the terrorists had to be stopped. In the summer of 2004, violence had flared across the South. It was summoned up by Moqtada al-Sadr, a radical young Shiite cleric, after a summons for his arrest for complicity in the murder of a rival cleric had been issued. In response, he had occupied the mosque in the holy city of Najaf and his militias tried to take control of several southern cities; after brutally intense firefights, the British stopped them. The revolt ended after the intervention of Ayatollah al-Sistani, who gave no support to al-Sadr's violent behavior.

More and more responsibility for security lay in the hands of the new Iraqi security forces—police, National Guard and soldiers. There were now about 96,000 in all—by the end of 2005, 234,000 were to be trained. They were not of uniformly high standard, and the terrorists were focusing attacks upon them. Al-Zarqawi had just issued another call to victory in which he warned, "The American army has begun to disappear from some cities. An Iraqi army has taken its place, and this is the real problem we face."

Everyone I met acknowledged that the Coalition had made serious mistakes. Disbanding the army, police, and intelligence services and purging the ministries too harshly of all members of the Baathist Party (rather than removing the worst) had probably created unnecessary confusion and lost much good will. The $18 billion pledged by Washington was still being spent too slowly, partly because of the lack of security, partly because of bureaucratic delays in Washington. Now $3 billion of it had to be diverted from water and electricity into security. The United Nations was still very wary of Iraq and almost none of its members had responded to the secretary general's request for troops to defend its vital electoral work. Shockingly, it sometimes seemed that even some of America's most significant allies (particularly in Europe) did not want the new Iraq to succeed.

General Mike Jackson, the British chief of general staff, said to me in Baghdad that the impression given by the media that the war was lost was, "Blatant hyperbole. Baghdad is not in flames. The insurgents do not represent the vast majority of Iraqis. They can be defeated. But it will take hard pounding."

Behind the grim headlines, life for the vast majority of the 25 million Iraqis was improving. Most of them were not being car-bombed. Children were back at school. (Almost 3,000 schools had been renovated.) The electricity grid was being rebuilt, was constantly blown up, and rebuilt again. Oil exports were rising, despite sabotage. Convoys of trucks were bringing in goods from Kuwait every day.

American troops at every rank seemed to be utterly committed to their tasks. Unlike Europeans, they saw this as an existential war. Casualties were growing all the time. By September 2004, 748 Americans had been killed and almost 7,000 wounded, but U.S. morale was high. I went to the U.S. headquarters in the International (or Green) Zone, where Lieutenant Dave Robison, a Texan doing guard duty at the heavily-fortified entrance to the Zone, spoke of the need to give Iraqis a chance. "I'm a tanker. If I had my first choice, I'd be out in the desert doing some Rommel-type stuff. But I'm glad to be helping." He talked also of the difficulty of stopping potential suicide bombers. "We can sometimes spot them because they have purified themselves by shaving their beards and hair and their cars are obviously very heavily loaded—often packed with artillery shells as well as high explosive." A few days before, a man had driven [the streets] to inflict his crime with a woman and two children in his car. I was told this was to disguise his purpose. All of them were blown to tiny pieces, along with innocent bystanders near where the car was detonated.

Inside one of Saddam's grotesque palaces, General David Petraeus, the 101st Airborne commander in charge of training Iraqi forces, affirmed that, "Iraq is more manageable on the inside than it seems in the media on the outside." He said working in Iraq was like being on a roller coaster: "It goes up and down but it's gradually climbing." General Thomas Metz, the U.S. Corps commander, had on his wall a collage of photographs of 9/11. In a quiet voice, he said, "The insurgents know that Iraq has a great future—it has water, oil, and a hard-working population."

A few weeks later, real American commitment was demanded in the postponed struggle to free Fallujah from the grip of the terrorists. The battle was led by the Marines. One officer, Lieutenant Colonel Dave Bellon, gave a graphic description of the fighting when he wrote home. He praised the courage of his soldiers but also acknowledged the ferocity of the men they were fighting.

> The enemy is willing to die and is literally waiting till they see the whites of the eyes of the Marines before they open up. Just two days ago, as a firefight raged at close quarters, one of the interpreters yelled for the enemy in the house

to surrender. They yelled back that it was better to die and go to heaven than to surrender to infidels.... One of the most amazing aspects to the fighting was that we saw virtually no civilians. Only after the fighting had passed did a few come out of their homes. They were provided food and water and most were evacuated from the city. At least 90-95 percent of the people were gone from the city when we attacked.

Even with everything that I knew and expected from the last nine months, the brutality and fanaticism of the enemy surprised me. The beheadings were even more commonplace than we thought, so were the torture and summary executions. Even though it is an exaggeration, it seems as though every block in the northern part of the city has a torture chamber or execution site. There are hundreds of tons of munitions and tens of thousands of weapons that our regiment alone has recovered. [We] have also found over 400 IEDs [improvised explosive devices] already wired and ready to detonate.... I know of several instances where near-dead enemy rolled grenades out on Marines who were prepared to aid them. It was a fight to the finish in every sense...

The Marines' victory in Fallujah cost the lives of Iraqi civilians as well as of terrorists and Marines themselves. But without removing this safe haven and command and control center from the terrorists, coalition and Iraqi troops could never have even begun to protect the bulk of voters in the January 2005 elections. Most U.S. commanders thought that it had been wrong to defer the task. But by the end of the year, Fallujah was no longer a safe haven.

The continuous backdrop to the slow but real progress of the U.S. troops in Iraq has been the debate on the origins of the war and, in particular, on the truth of Saddam's much-vaunted and much-feared Weapons of Mass Destruction, the principal casus belli. A 511-page report by the Senate Intelligence Committee had, in rather broad brush terms, described a "global intelligence failure."

In October 2004, Charles Duelfer, the leader of the Iraq Survey Group, presented his *Comprehensive Report* on the WMD issue. He had already said in an interim report to Congress that he had had great difficulty persuading key people in Iraq to speak. "On one hand there is a fear of prosecution or arrest. On the other there is a fear former regime supporters will exact retribution."

He had pointed out that strict compartmentalization is a feature of such despotic regimes—Stalin's atom bomb program was run for years by his police chief, Lavrenti Beria, and most senior military and political leaders knew nothing of it.

So it was under Saddam. According to Duelfer's earlier

testimony, "We know from high-level debriefings that Saddam conveyed his most sensitive messages to particular individuals orally. Moreover, there were explicit instructions not to repeat such conversations."

Duelfer told Congress that Iraq's illegal military procurement budget increased 100-fold, from 1996 to 2003, to $500 million, most of the money coming from illicit oil contracts. "Iraq imported banned military weapons and technology and dual-use goods through Oil for Food contracts." Duelfer and his team also provided the oil export data and Oil for Food information from the Saddam era. These data presented a compelling picture of the objectives and methods of the Regime. It was clear Saddam had been buying influence in the UN and around the world to support his goal of eroding sanctions. It was also clear that his ambitions for Iraq included renewing his WMD.

In his *Comprehensive Report*, Duelfer stated that he had not been able to find the stockpiles of banned biological and chemical weapons that were thought, before the invasion, to be concealed in Iraq. However, he did not conclude that sanctions had worked. Instead he stated that, "By 2000–2001, Saddam had managed to mitigate many of the effects of sanctions and undermine their international support. Iraq was within striking distance of a de facto end to the sanctions regime."

He confirmed that Saddam was convinced that WMD were essential to preserving his power. Perhaps in order to deter his hostile neighbor Iran, he had engaged in strategic deception designed to suggest that he retained his weapons and he fully intended to resume real WMD production after the expected lifting of UN sanctions. Duelfer showed that he had maintained weapons programs that put him in material breach of UN resolutions, including 1441. And Saddam had set up a vast bribery scheme, aimed primarily at three of the five permanent members of the Security Council—China, France and Russia—with the intent of having them help lift those sanctions.

"Saddam personally approved and removed all names of voucher recipients under the Oil-for-Food program," Duelfer wrote. The alleged beneficiaries of such bribes included individuals in China as well as some with close ties to President Putin of Russia and President Chirac of France. Duelfer uncovered one Iraqi intelligence report which stated that French politicians had assured Saddam in writing that France would use its UN veto against any U.S. effort to attack Iraq—in March 2003 France threatened to do just that. Duelfer wrote "politically the Iraqis were losing their stigma" by 2001.

Intelligence is a craft and intelligence agencies have to make judgements on the basis of past behavior, current evidence (even if limited), and future planning. Given all we knew of Saddam by 2003, the conclusion had to be that he still possessed a residual WMD capacity and that he was determined to restore his original capabilities; but it was not possible to determine how far development had gone. There was no doubt that Saddam's plans for WMD constituted, in the words of one intelligence official, an iceberg ahead. We saw the tip of the iceberg, but we did not know how deep or wide it was. We only eventually came to be certain that Saddam no longer had stockpiles of weapons in 2003 because of regime change. Before that there was just no way of knowing the truth.

The Duelfer report appeared at the same time as *The Bomb in My Garden*, a book by Dr. Mahdi Obeidi, Saddam's chief nuclear physicist. Obeidi's book showed the climate of terror in which Saddam had pursued WMD. He had been forced to work in Saddam's nuclear program—with his family held hostage. He showed how simple it was to obtain components for nuclear devices on the world market and he recounted that after the invasion of Kuwait, Saddam's thugs tried to compel Iraqi scientists to produce a single "dirty" nuclear device at once. Fortunately they could not do so.

On the orders of Saddam's son Qusay, Dr. Obeidi buried in his own garden a large barrel containing the parts of a centrifuge for enriching uranium and all the instructions needed for that. When interviewed by UN weapons inspectors in the 1990s, Obeidi naturally made no mention of the bomb in his garden. Only after Saddam was gone did he reveal the truth. He concluded that if Saddam had been allowed to escape once more in 2003, and had sanctions been lifted as his French, Russian, and Chinese friends had wished, Saddam would have started again. "Our nuclear program could have been reconstituted at the snap of Saddam Hussein's fingers," he wrote. "Iraqi scientists had the knowledge and the designs need to jumpstart the program if necessary."

The combination of international terror and WMD poses an existential threat to the survival of free societies. We are fighting a third world war. In the case of Iraq, the possibility of a non-conventional attack might by 2003 have been low, but the price to be paid, had one occurred, would have been enormous. A rogue state which reconstitutes its WMD arsenal in its own time (as Iraq could have done if sanctions had been lifted) poses the same level of threat as a regime already in possession of WMD. In the case of Iraq, as in so many other cases, a difficult decision had to be made on the basis of imperfect and ambiguous intelligence.

Saddam Hussein was, at the very least, clearly determined that the world remain uncertain about his WMD program. By frustrating the UN inspectors, he encouraged suspicion. His entire rule was based on lies and double-dealing. So the claim that he had a clandestine weapons program was entirely plausible.

If the CIA and MI6 had in fact reported in 2003 that Iraq was genuinely free of WMDs, the nature of the Baathist regime would not have changed. Saddam would still have destabilized the Middle East. His regime would have continued to be a daily disaster for the Iraqi people. If the UN had been compelled to lift sanctions on Iraq, as Saddam's friends in Paris, Moscow, Beijing, and elsewhere were urging, his regime would have been greatly strengthened and would have become a greater threat, much harder to destroy. The regime's failure to accept the last chance to be seen to disarm, as offered by Resolution 1441 of November 2002, showed that Saddam would never relinquish his WMD ambitions and that they could be ended only by regime change.

Instead of attacking George Bush, Tony Blair, John Howard, Jose Maria Aznar, and their allies for the failure to find chemical and biological weapons, the critics should have tried to imagine the consequences if Iraq had in fact been as advanced along this road as North Korea, or even Iran. Despite their critics' assertions, Bush and Blair did not lie when they said they believed that Saddam still had WMD.

That belief was general. General Tommy Franks, the U.S. Commander in Iraq during the invasion, has revealed that both King Abdullah of Jordan and President Mubarak of Egypt told him before the war that they were convinced that Saddam had WMD. U.S. military commanders fully expected him to deploy chemical weapons against their troops.

As Charles Duelfer pointed out to this author, "In democracies it is very hard to make strategic decisions. The pressures of elections and budgets compress evaluations of costs and benefit. Horizons are very short. But Saddam had the freedom to act strategically. He had had over a decade in which he had seen how hard it was for the international community to agree to take decisive action against him. Unlike Bush and Blair, he had no problems of building public or political support. He could sustain a WMD goal and regional ambitions of great menace until the most propitious moment for him."

Duelfer continued, "Blix's inspections may have been working in the short term, but the underlying dynamics were not good for international security. There was never going to be a good moment for military action to depose him. But the combination of Saddam, Iraq, and WMD expertise was one that could not be managed forever."

The truth is that neither Iraq nor the region had any hope of progress so long as Iraq was ruled by Saddam Hussein, the most brutal dictator of modern times. Iraqis themselves were unable to overthrow him because in his "Republic of Fear," economic and military power were controlled by him and his ruthless sons. This gangster family had shown itself prepared to go to any lengths, including using chemical weapons against a whole town, to crush opposition and perpetuate its rule.

Their regime was an equal danger to the region. Saddam had initiated two major wars. He had tried to wipe a member state of the United Nations off the map. He had triggered an arms race in the Gulf. His ambitions were feared by all those same neighbors who, hypocritically, denounced the Coalition for removing him.

Before the invasion there was what Lord Butler, who headed an important British inquiry into the reasons for the invasion, called a "creeping tide" of WMD proliferation. It included also Iran, Libya, and Syria, as well as North Korea. Efraim Halevy, the former head of MOSSAD, said in his 2004 Portland Trust Lecture in London, "The region was in danger of becoming saturated with rogue or dictatorial regimes and no-state groups hurtling towards nuclear and other non-conventional fulfilment. If things were left as they were, the situation could well get out of control."

The conditions that led Saddam to defer his WMD ambitions were not sustainable over the long term. Were we to bet our long-term security on the resilience of the Security Council remaining tough on Iraqi compliance? Duelfer revealed the way in which even members of the Security Council undertook extensive covert transactions with Iraq, in direct violation of the resolutions they had passed.

The historian Philip Bobbitt has pointed out, "It cannot be better to avoid action until we are certain that the situation we most fear has indeed come about." Saddam may not have been an immediate threat but he was certainly an inevitable one. And, after 9/11, an intolerable one.

Critics of the American presence in Iraq seemed unable to recognize the realities of the Middle East. John Kerry, the Democratic candidate in the 2004 U.S. presidential election, denounced the intervention in Iraq as "wrong war, wrong place, wrong time." He attacked the alliance as a "trumped-up, so-called coalition of the bribed, the coerced, the bought, and the extorted." He said, "When they talk about a coalition, that's the phoniest thing I've ever heard. You've got 500 troops here, 500 troops there, and it's American troops that are 90 percent of the combat casualties and it's American taxpayers that are paying 90 percent of the cost of the war." Kerry charged that Bush had misled the American people.

In January 2005, a prominent Iraqi trade union leader, Haadi Salih, was abducted, tied up, blindfolded, and tortured by Baathist terrorists loyal to Saddam Hussein. He was then strangled by electric cord and shot dead. There was very little horror expressed by the antiwar movement in either North America or Europe.

The self-righteous critics of Bush, Blair, Berlusconi, and John Howard were simply not prepared to recognize that Saddam's regime was fascistic in both philosophy and practice, and a threat far beyond Iraq itself. They would not see that, apart from removing the threat of a Saddam Hussein armed beyond deterrence, there were other bold elements in Bush's strategy. The challenge to a ruthless outlaw government in the most strategically important country in the Middle East was hugely ambitious. It was intended to change the whole nature of the region. And slowly it seemed to begin to work, threatening the area's worst vested interests. That was why there was so much opposition to it.

In the international area, the removal of Saddam led to the closing of a secret Pakistani black market in nuclear materials and expertise. It also led the Libyan dictator, Muammar Gaddafi, to renounce his own weapons of mass destruction and to bring his country back into the international system after decades of imposing and pursuing terrorism both at home and abroad. This fundamental change did not change the domestic nature of Gadaffi's regime, but it did remove another serious threat to the international system. A nuclear-armed Gaddafi would have been as dangerous as a nuclear-armed Saddam; now neither was a possibility.

There were other reverberations throughout the Arab world, helped by the serendipitous death of Yasser Arafat. In a complete reversal of American policy, Bush had decided in his first term to have no truck with Arafat. Previous U.S. presidents, in particular Clinton, had built not only the road map but their entire Middle Eastern policy around the Palestinian leader. This was despite the fact that Arafat had done more than any other single leader to perpetuate the politics of despair in the Middle East. Five wars and two intifadas: the corrupt, cruelly unrealistic leadership of Arafat, in which everything was blamed upon Israel, had achieved nothing for the Palestinians.

Bush, by contrast, encouraged the Palestinians to move away from the politics of victimhood and toward reality. At the same time he gave Israel enough sense of security to enable it to make concessions—which Ariel Sharon, one of the most controversial but probably most significant Israeli leaders in recent history, embarked upon.

In January 2005, the Palestinian Authority ran elections, the first in nine years, to choose a successor to Arafat.

Turnout was immense, the polls were not blighted by killings and could be said to be more free than any they had held before. They chose Mahmoud Abbas, who had pledged to try and work with Israel and control extremist violence in ways which Arafat had never deigned to do.

In Lebanon, the former Prime Minister Rafik Hariri, a popular figure leading the opposition to Syrian occupation, was assassinated in a massive car bomb, almost certainly organized by Syrian agents. This unleashed pent-up fury in the country. Hundreds of thousands of protestors took to the streets to demand the end of Syria's control of Lebanon.

None of this would have happened had the Allies not broken the logjam by removing Saddam. The young Lebanese in the streets of Beirut knew that they had the backing of Bush. Indeed some held up placards which read, "Thank you, Bush." By the beginning of March, the pro-Syrian Lebanese government had fallen and the Syrians had begun to withdraw their troops, a process which was said to have been completed before the end of April.

The Lebanese Druze leader, Walid Jumblatt, long a critic of the United States, declared, "It is strange for me to say it, but this process of change has started because of the American invasion of Iraq. I was cynical about Iraq. But when I saw the Iraqi people voting three weeks ago, 8 million of them, it was the start of a new Arab world. The Syrian peo-

ple, the Egyptian people, all say that something is changing. The Berlin Wall has fallen. We can see it."

In Saudi Arabia and Egypt also, change was coming. The
Saudis allowed the first local elections in the country's history. It was true that only men were allowed to vote and
the councils which they were electing could not make
important decisions. But it was a start and, in Saudi terms,
almost revolutionary. In Egypt, President Mubarak, under
strong U.S. pressure, decided to finally allow opponents to
run against him in the next presidential election. Although
he was unlikely to lose, there was some reason to hope
that, perhaps in Cairo, the Arab custom of turning dictatorships into dynasties would come to an end.

The success of the Iraq election did not alone guarantee
the future and security of the country, but it did change the
nature of the debate around the world. Until then, Western
critics and Middle Eastern opponents of the U.S.-led intervention felt able to claim (however speciously) that the terrorists in Iraq were "resistance to American occupation."
No longer.

Some Middle Eastern commentators maintained that
the elections were the most important event in modern
Arab history since Nasser's defeat by Israel in the 1967 6-day
war. Al Jazeera found itself in an odd position. Hitherto, it
had broadcast hate-filled images of the American occupa-

tion of Iraq to the region and had tried to convince its viewers around the world that the terrorists represented the real Iraq. The elections gave the lie to this. Al Jazeera's editorial policy was fiercely opposed to the U.S. intervention, but its pictures now showed 8 million Arabs voting more freely than Arabs anywhere. Viewers in Saudi Arabia, Yemen, Egypt, and Algeria could see whole families of Iraqis walking with purpose to the polling booths and then proudly displaying their fingers stained with ink.

In Syria, citizens watched Iraqi exiles there voting in elections far freer than their government had ever allowed them to take part in. The government-controlled media attempted to pretend that nothing had happened. But satellite television coverage of voting in Iraq made that impossible.

The Iraqi daily *Al-Mada* wrote in an editorial headlined "Now. . . Not Tomorrow", "Who could have expected this popular victory under the Iraqi conditions, conditions of occupation, the blowing up of children and cars, mortar fire and assassinations, and then the threat 'to wash the streets of Baghdad with the blood of voters' which appeared in a terrorist statement distributed on the eve of the elections?"

Al-Zaman, published in both London and Baghdad, declared, "The success which characterized the elections is not a monopoly of one list or a limited number of lists;

instead it is a success for all the lists and thus for all Iraqis. There are no winners or losers in adopting national values."

The London-based *Al-Hayat* wrote in its editorial, "The scene of elections, ballot boxes, voters, the competition between parties and lists [of candidates], the election campaign and counter-campaign, and the guarantee of the women's share in the [National Assembly] seats transmit joy to the heart." As well as praising the courage of the Iraqi people, the paper pointed out, "What we have seen in occupied Iraq is more advanced than what we know in the independent and liberated Arab countries. The respectable average participation in the voting has, despite everything, rendered those who resist the new circumstances less legitimate—and ultimately closer to terrorism than to resistance."

All over the Arab world (except in the government-controlled papers) the enthusiasm was similar. The Saudi daily *Al-Watan* wrote that despite all the events surrounding them, the elections "have revealed great Iraqi enthusiasm for democracy and the innate perception by the Iraqis, particularly amongst the simple folk, of the importance of participating in charting the characteristics of the future." One Saudi columnist, Dr. Mohammad T. al-Rasheed wrote effusively, "Bravo Iraq! For history, January 30, 2005 is one magnificent day for Iraq and the Arab nation. Regardless of who won or lost, the day should be a permanent fixture on the

Arab calendar forever. I don't want to talk politics; I simply want to celebrate history. Despite everything, the Iraqis voted. They did so with a passion and a seriousness that gives the lie to the cliché that Arabs are not ready for democracy."

In France, even President Chirac acknowledged that the election was "an important stage in the political reconstruction of Iraq" and that "the strategy of terrorist groups [had] partly failed." France had previously described the insurgents as "our friends."

In the U.S., Senator Kerry was dismissive: "No one should over-hype the results of this election," he opined. This was a minority view. Even Senator Edward Kennedy, a bitter critic of the invasion, admitted that President Bush might deserve credit "for what seemed to be a tentative awakening of democracy in the region." Senator Hillary Rodham Clinton, whose attitude toward Iraq had been more sophisticated and sympathetic than most leading Democrats, acknowledged in 2005, "There can be no doubt that it is not in America's interests for the Iraqi government, the experiment in freedom and democracy, to fail. So I hope that Americans understand that and that we will have as united a front as is possible in [the] country at this time to keep our troops safe, make sure they have everything they need, and try to support this new Iraqi government."

Charles Krauthammer, a columnist often dubbed "neoconservative," wrote in *Time* magazine, "What changed the climate in the Middle East was not just the U.S. invasion and show of arms. It was U.S. determination and staying power, and the refusal of its people last November to turn out a president who rejected an 'exit strategy.'" The implications of giving Kurds and Shia parity with the Sunni minority which hitherto had dominated and persecuted them would have profound implications not only in Iraq itself but also throughout the Sunni-dominated Arab world. The historian Victor Davis Hanson suggested that American sponsorship of the traditional underclass in the Middle East was "one of the most radical social and cultural upheavals since the American-sponsored emancipation of women in post-war Japan or our own civil rights movement of the 1960s."

Krauthammer also pointed out that the liberal left, both in America and in Europe was, quite simply, shown to be morally bankrupt by the courage of the Iraqi people. It was Republican Bush who demanded that the tyranny of Saddam finally end, and the Iraqi people who took the opportunity offered.

In the *Washington Post*, Jim Hoagland emphasized the extraordinary fact that nearly a third of the 140 winning candidates on Iraq's Shiite parliamentary list are women. But women's liberationists in the West seemed reluctant to publicize this extraordinary revolution. "Could they not want to accept even implicitly the notion that war can create the conditions needed for a positive social revolution?" asked Hoagland.

The answer to his question was clear: many Western liberals could not acknowledge the revolution that, despite many setbacks, was taking place. Inside Iraq, USAID continued to give assistance to women's and other groups in ways to develop civil society. As just one example, in late March 2005, women active in the new political system attended a two-day seminar on the basics of public speaking and political party advancement.

The Iraqi minister of human rights, Bakhtiar Amin, a Kurd, told Roger Cohen of the *International Herald Tribune*, "We owe our freedom to Americans. The real occupation is not theirs but the one we suffered for thirty-five years by the group of thugs who brutalized my nation." Cohen wrote that there were far too many horror stories "for the Germans and the French to be comfortable in their conviction that the war was wrong. The war was falsely portrayed, poorly planned and hurt by hubris. But it was the right war."

In London, the *Independent*, fiercely against the Iraq War, asked, "Was Bush right after all?" In Germany, *Der Spiegel*, the top news weekly, published an article which dared suggest that people in the Middle East "will get the idea in their heads to free themselves from their oppressive regimes just as the East Germans did. Just a thought for Old Europe to chew on: Bush might be right, just like Reagan was."

Bush himself did not claim the credit. But in March 2005 he did say, "The advance of hope in the Middle East requires new thinking in the region. By now it should be clear that authoritarian rule is not the wave of the future; it is the last gasp of a discredited past.... By now it should be clear that decades of excusing and accommodating tyranny, in the pursuit of stability, have led only to injustice, instability and tragedy."

Behind the headlines, much of Iraq stepped forward, even as the bombers tried to blast it back.

Work on both the physical and the political infrastructure was continually disrupted by terrorist attacks. But, despite the continuing insecurity, Baghdad real estate prices were increasing and in some districts homes were now four times as valuable as in 2003. The stock exchange was still tiny, but it was expanding, as was foreign investment. Chambers of Commerce were being established and USAID offered training in commercial, maritime and international law, information technology, assessment of infrastructure needs, building databases—and much more besides. Attacks on oil pipelines and plants were still deterring vitally needed foreign investment in this sector, but initial talks with seventeen international companies about the construction of a new refinery had been successful, and production in the southern fields was now up to pre-war levels, despite sabotage.

Direct flights between Beirut and Kurdistan on Magic Carpet Airlines had joined those to Amman and Dubai. Rail services from Mosul to other cities had resumed. The State Department had recognized that the pace of reconstruction had been damaged by the early decision to hire U.S. companies for major reconstruction projects. Some major projects had been cancelled and were being re-tendered to Iraqi companies.

There was another important effect: the impact on economic growth in the whole area. After Saddam's overthrow, every major capital index in the Middle East rose; regional stock markets rose 30 percent in 2004. The Egyptian equity index went up by 165 percent, while Saudi Arabia's went up by 158 percent. In Iraq itself a new Stock Exchange and an independent securities commission were established. Saddam had mortgaged the country to fund his tyranny and his pretensions. By 2003 Iraq's estimated external debt was $129 billion—about 350 percent of GDP, a huge stumbling block to its development, which the U.S. took the lead in trying to get reduced. By early 2005, former Secretary of State James Baker had made the rounds of the principal creditors, and had helped persuade the creditors to write down some $80-$90 billion of the total indebtedness.

Fallujah was still wrecked, with many of its residents camping outside the town as refugees in tents. But the Ministry of Municipality and Works had invested $800,000 in repairing eight pumping stations and rebuilding the infrastructure of the ravaged town. Hospitals, clinics, and schools were being restored. About $500 million was being spent on reconstruction in and around Samarra. In its rural water initiative, USAID was working in seventy-four different sites. The Ministry of Education was setting up a new education television channel to broadcast six hours a day, seven days a week. (There had once been an educational channel under Saddam, but in 1993 his son Uday removed its equipment to start his own channel.) On April 2, a massive new generator, weighing 700 tons, reached its destination, Kirkuk, traveling at 5 mph under heavy U.S. military escort 640 miles from Jordan. It was part of a countrywide USAID project to bring reliable power to the national grid. One could of course wish that it had arrived in summer 2003 instead of spring 2005.

The game was not won. In Iraq itself, Abu Musab al-Zarqawi continued to evade capture by U.S. troops. Both his Islamic terrorists and "former regime elements" were still determined to derail all progress, and the violence continued in its horribly predictable manner. One car bomb at the end of February murdered 125 people in the town of al-Hillah, south of Baghdad. Some of the dead were police recruits. Others were women and children at the local market.

After the election, the creation of a new government took almost three months—so long that some Western opponents of the new Iraq claimed that the spirit of political compromise was inimical to the region. Equally, the long period of gestation could be taken as evidence that, confronted with the freedom to create political compromises for the first time ever, Iraq's leaders applied themselves diligently to the task. Coalition politics is not simple anywhere; in Iraq, as the analyst Amir Taheri pointed out, it was further complicated because the two big winning blocs, the Shia and the Kurds, were themselves coalitions.

The first task was to choose a Prime Minister. There were four possible candidates; at one point all the groups asked al-Sistani to choose. He refused, because he thought the new leadership must remain accountable to the electorate. Eventually Ibrahim al-Ja'afari, a 58-year-old doctor and devout Shiite, was chosen as a compromise candidate.

Then the debate began over filling other cabinet posts. It was not easy. The Kurds insisted on retaining a right of veto under any future constitution. They insisted on retaining their own army, the "Peshmerga" and they continued to press their claim to Kirkuk, an oil-rich border town which Saddam had ethnically cleansed of Kurds and refilled with Arabs.

On April 28, most members of the new government were finally agreed upon by the parliament elected in January. It was a moment of great significance. Iraq now had the first popularly-elected government in its history and the only such government in the Arab world. Its success would depend much more on the Iraqis themselves than on anything the United States could do for it, beyond trying to enhance its security.

The Shia and Kurdish alliances both realized the need to persuade the Sunnis to take part in the democratic adventure. Sunnis were given seven positions in the new government. Still, Sunni terrorists continued to do everything they could to create chaos. Hundreds more were killed. In mid-April Marla Ruzicka, a 28-year-old American woman who had become a heroine in both Afghanistan and Iraq for her work in demanding the U.S. assist innocent civilian victims of conflict, was murdered by a suicide bomber. A few days later, another brave woman, Sheikha Lameah Khaddouri, a member of parliament, was repeatedly shot in her face and chest. She was the first of the eighty-nine women in the new parliament to be killed. At the end of April the carnage increased; the terrorists mounted more and more suicide attacks, every day killing as many people as they could manage. On April 30, suicide bombers killed another fifteen people, and three civilians in Falluja were killed by rockets launched by the terrorists. One of the suicide bombs in Baghdad was aimed at a Sunni political leader in talks with the new government. Sunni terrorists declared that they would kill any Sunni who participated. The offices of another Sunni group were bombed and four of its staff were killed or wounded—it withdrew from the government. Over the three days of the first weekend of May, more than 100 Iraqis were killed and another 200 wounded in the relentless attempts to undermine the new government. On May 4, over fifty people were murdered and up to 150 wounded by a suicide bomber in the Kurdish town of Irbil in northern Iraq. And so it went on, day after day.

By the middle of May, over 400 Iraqis had been murdered by the Baathists and Islamic Fundamentalists. Most of the victims were Shiite and Kurdish civilians–women, children, men—shopping, on the way to the mosque, or lining up to join the security forces.

On May 18, a chilling new audio message, apparently

from al-Zarqawi, was posted on Islamic websites. It claimed that the murder of innocent Muslims was justified. "The shedding of Muslim blood. . . is allowed in order to avoid the greater evil of disrupting jihad. . ." The terrorist leader defended suicide attacks, saying, "killing of infidels by any method, including martyrdom operations, has been sanctified by many scholars even if it meant killing innocent Muslims. . . . This legality has been agreed upon. . . so as not to disrupt jihad. . ."

Even more shocking than such attempts to justify the relentless carnage was the lack of protest at the mass murders around the world, particularly in the Islamic world. As Tom Friedman noted in the *New York Times*, "I have not read of a single fatwa issued by any Muslim cleric outside Iraq condemning these indiscriminate mass murders of Iraqi Shiites and Kurds by these jihadist suicide bombers. . ." Sunni fundamentalists and Baathist terrorists do not consider Shiites real Muslims, and are indifferent to their fate. And several Arab regimes—perhaps Syria in particular—are actively encouraging and supporting the bloodshed in Iraq in order to stop the spread of democratization to themselves.

Despite all such assaults, on May 8, Prime Minister al-Ja'afari completed his cabinet, having found Sunnis to take up prominent positions, including a Sunni Minister of

Defense. There had been fears that the new government would be dominated by Iran, since al-Ja'afari had long term ties to that country. But with the president a Kurd, this danger seemed remote. The greater risk was that the Sunni insurgents would redouble their terrorist campaign to force all Sunnis to stop co-operating with the authorities.

In the long-term, it seems clear that the insurgency can and will be defeated. But it will take continued courage and continued persistence, above all on the part of the Iraqi people, the new Iraqi security forces, and the men and women of the U.S. armed forces. Much *can* still go wrong, but more than two years after the invasion and despite the horror-filled headlines, Iraq is a place of hope as well as danger and fragility. The good news should be getting at least as much attention as the continuing atrocities.

Iraq's 25 million people possess the world's second largest reserves of oil and their country is the only one in the Middle East with sufficient water resources to sustain a major agricultural economy. What the jihadists and the despots of the region know (and fear) is that if any Arab country has the chance of becoming a prosperous and pluralist society in the foreseeable future, it is Iraq. The instruments of despotism have been removed in Iraq, if not entirely destroyed. A free press, trade unions, political parties, and associations flourish. A remarkable, confidence-building election has taken place.

To mark the second anniversary of Saddam's fall, the BBC broadcast interviews with seven Iraqis on how life had changed for them. The Australian blogger, Arthur Chrenkoff, who reported these interviews in his invaluable regular series "Good news from Iraq" (www.chrenkoff.blogspot.com), noted that "the results were surprising, certainly for the BBC, whose attitude towards the liberation of Iraq has always been at best lukewarm."

Saad, 32, a sound engineer from Basra, said, "Iraqis are feeling better. They are breathing the air of freedom. They read, watch and say what they want. They travel, work and receive a living wage. They use mobile phones, satellite dishes and the internet, which they did not even know before... As for terrorism, we are now beginning to unite against it and to defeat it."

Noura, 32, a computer engineer from Baghdad and a Christian: "While we lost security after Saddam's fall, we gained our freedom and a chance to build a new society."

Nada, 32, a government worker from Mosul: "We never imagined that the Turkmen community would have a political party representing them in Iraq, but this is happening now."

Kaban, 31, an engineer from Baghdad, said, "Those who say that security was better in the past are completely wrong. It is true we did not have suicide bombings in Saddam's era, but our homes did not feel safe from the intrusion of Saddam's security men, who came in the middle of the night, to kidnap, kill, or rape."

Waala, 25, a school teacher from Baghdad: "The Sunnis in Iraq do not live in isolation from the political and social circles of life, as many people outside Iraq seem to believe. Nothing has affected our relationships with each other— we face the same problems. This applies to Sunnis or Shia, Christians or Muslims, Arabs or Kurds. Unfortunately, the refusal by some Sunnis to participate in the elections was the cause of some political isolation."

Imad Mohammed, 25, a graduate from Baghdad: "I am no longer worried about losing my dignity or my life. And I am also getting a higher income, like most Iraqis."

The human costs continue to be tragic. The most authoritative website on Iraqi civilian casualties—www. iraqbodycount.com—suggested that at least 20,000 Iraqi civilians had been killed since March 2003. Some estimates said more. By May 2005, over 1,600 Americans had been killed and at least 24,700 had been wounded. The terrorists hoped that this continual bloodletting would erode public support in America and build up Arab support for the anti-democratic cause. In fact, in the weeks following the election, the opposite seems to have occurred. Far more Arab commentators and even states saw the Iraqi elections as a harbinger of the future.

The continuing slaughter unleashed by the terrorists was nihilistic. It was designed to try and provoke civil war and to deny the Iraqis the chance of creating a civil society. They had nothing to offer. They were able to summon up more and more lone killers prepared to strap belts of explosives around themselves or to drive cars laden with gelignite. But suicide bombing was now their principal tactic and it was the principal metaphor for the opposition to the new Iraq. It was not an inspiring clarion call.

Since the election, many more Iraqis brought the government forces information which led to the arrest or deaths of many terrorists. Al-Zarqawi himself narrowly escaped arrest in April, and a letter from one of his associates was discovered which complained that "morale is weakening" and that "the situation is not the way it used to be in Fallujah."

After the appointment of the Sunni minister of defense, Iraq papers reported that Sunnis in Baghdad began to apply in large numbers to join the security services. On May 9, U.S. Marines mounted a major attack on insurgent bases near the Syrian border.

It would be foolish to say that any corner has yet been turned or that there is, in the phrase made famous in Vietnam, "light at the end of the tunnel." But it is clear that soldiers from the United States, Britain, Italy, Poland,

Australia, and many other countries have achieved a great deal since 9/11.

Afghanistan has been given a completely new start and all its people, especially its woman, now have opportunities of enjoying civil society that they have never had before. The same is true of Iraq, though the fascistic rearguard action of resistance to change is far stronger and more brutal there. The effects of the elections in both Afghanistan and Iraq are unsettling regimes and inspiring people across the region.

The critics of Bush and Blair refuse to recognize this. Blair was much abused for Iraq during the May 2005 election campaign in Britain. He nonetheless won the election, as had George Bush and John Howard of Australia, two other anti-Saddam leaders, before him.

Martin Gilbert, the official biographer of Winston Churchill, had a different view. He suggested that Bush and Blair's efforts to transform the Middle East may one day be accorded the same historical stature as Roosevelt and Churchill. The two victors of the Second World War defeated Nazism and shaped the post-war world for the better. George Bush, Tony Blair, and their allies have embarked on a difficult but essential war against despotism, Islamic and secular, in the world's most dangerous region.

It seems astonishing that more people in the West do

not recognize the nature of the struggle taking place. The Coalition is not faced by a coherent "insurgency," still less a "resistance" movement with a national cause or political program. On the contrary, they are fighting gangs of theocratic and fascistic murderers who have nothing to offer but more murder. They deserve support from no one.

I repeat, serious mistakes have been made by the Coalition during the last two years. Even so, thanks above all to the sacrifice of young Americans and to the courage of the Iraqis, the possibilities of a better future for Iraq, and indeed for all the peoples of the area, are immense.

LONDON, MAY 16, 2005

A NOTE ON THE SOURCES

I have plundered a great many books by other authors for this short work. Among the books I have used, and to whose authors I express my great gratitude, are:

Richard Butler, *Saddam Defiant* (London: Weidenfeld and Nicholson, 2000). Originally published as *The Greatest Threat: Iraq, Weapons of Mass Destruction, and the Growing Crisis of Global Security* (New York: PublicAffairs, 2000).

Con Coughlin, *Saddam* (London: Macmillan, 2002).

Bernard Lewis, *What Went Wrong* (London: Weidenfeld and Nicolson, 2002).

Judith Miller, Stephen Engelberg, and William Broad, *Germs* (New York: Simon and Schuster, 2001).

Kenneth M. Pollack, *The Threatening Storm: The Case for Invading Iraq* (New York: Random House, 2002).

Roger Scruton, *The West and the Rest* (London: Continuum, 2002).

Peter Stothard, *30 Days: A Month at the Heart of Blair's War* (London: HarperCollins, 2003).

INTRODUCTION

Barham Saleh on Iraq as nexus, Neil MacFarquhar, *New York Times*, August 12, 2003.

CHAPTER I: THE GATE OF FIRE

Peggy Noonan on terrorists and the United States, *Forbes*, November 30, 1998, reprinted in *The Times* (London), October 16, 2001.

Eliza Manningham Buller remarks on terrorist threats, speech to Royal United Services Institute, London, June 17, 2003.

Bernard Lewis on Islam, *What Went Wrong* (London: Weidenfeld & Nicholson, 2002), p. 159.

Halabja, Kenneth M. Pollack, *The Threatening Storm: The Case for Invading Iraq* (New York: Random House, 2002), p. 23; Jeffrey Goldberg, *The New Yorker*, March 25, 2002.

Iran-Iraq war, see Con Coughlin, *Saddam* (London: Macmillan, 2002), and Pollack, op. cit.

Schwarzkopf and Iraqi surrender. Quoted by Christopher Hitchens, *Vanity Fair*, June 2003. See also Stephen F. Hayes,

Weekly Standard, March 10, 2003. The story is dealt with at length in Michael Gordon and Bernard E. Trainor, *The Generals' War* (Boston: Little, Brown, 1994). Schwarzkopf said later, "It had never crossed my mind that I'd have to sit down opposite Iraqi generals—and we spent a couple minutes discussing how this might be arranged." The president gave the CINC only forty-eight hours to prepare for the meeting. Powell directed Schwarzkopf to prepare "terms of reference" for the meeting. The CINC spent an hour dictating the terms, focusing exclusively on immediate military issues. He sought immediate release of all Coalition prisoners of war; exchange of information on people missing in action; return of the remains of people killed in action; and exchange of information on mines and booby traps, as well as on any storage sites the enemy had established for weapons of mass destruction in the Kuwait theater of operations. He also sought to establish a demarcation line to physically separate the Coalition and Iraqi armies. He transmitted the draft document to Washington, where the Joint Chiefs and State Department reviewed and approved it.

U.S. views on leaving Saddam in power, Pollack, op. cit., pp 46–54.

Charles Duelfer's views, interview with author, January 21, 2003.

Sanctions and Iraqi propaganda, Pollack, op. cit., pp 125–140; Martin Woollacott, *The Guardian* (London), February 23, 2001.

Horrors of Saddam's rule, Stephen F. Hayes, *Weekly Standard*, March 10, 2003.

CHAPTER 2: PRESIDENT BUSH AND PRIME MINISTER BLAIR

Bush's radicalism and his Christianity; see, for example, Bill Keller, *New York Times Magazine*, January 26, 2003; David Frum, *The Right Man* (New York: Random House, 2003), pp 24–25, 252–253.

Neoconservatives' history, see Peter Steinfels, *The Neoconservatives* (New York: Simon and Schuster, 1979); Joshua Muravchik, "The Neo-Conservative Cabal," *Commentary*, September 2003.

Bush on the wonderworking power of the American people, see Fritz Ritsch, "Of God, and Man, in the Oval Office," *Washington Post*, March 2, 2003.

Blair's views, see Peter Stothard, *30 Days: A Month at the Heart of Blair's War* (London: HarperCollins, 2003), passim; James Blitz, *Financial Times Magazine*, April 26, 2003.

Blair and Kosovo and Sierra Leone, see William Shawcross, *Deliver Us from Evil* (New York: Simon and Schuster, 2000), chap. 14.

Neo conservatives' background, see, for example, Tom Barry and Jim Lobe, "U.S. Foreign Policy: Attention, Right Face, Forward March," *Foreign Policy in Focus*, April 2002; John C. Hulsman, David Polansky, and Rachel Prager, "The Rebirth of Realism: The Kantian Trap—Utopianism in International Affairs," *National Interest*, vol. 1, no. 10, November 13, 2002

Rebuttal of criticisms of neoconservatives, see Joshua Muravchik, *Commentary*, September 2003, and Robert Lieber, "The Neoconservative Conspiracy Theory: Pure Myth," *Chronicle of Higher Education*, May 2, 2003.

David Frum on axis of evil, Frum, op. cit., pp. 224–245.

History of U.S. preeminence, see Lawrence Kaplan and William Kristol, *The War over Iraq: Saddam's Tyranny and America's Mission* (San Francisco: Encounter Books, 2002).

Justice Department's 1962 legal opinion, quoted in David Rivkin Jr. and Lee A. Casey, "Leashing the Dogs of War," *National Interest*, Fall 2003, pp. 57–69.

Philip Bobbitt, *The Times* (London), January 10, 2003.

Israel and Osirak reactor, see Coughlin, op. cit., p 189, and Pollack, op. cit., pp. 173, 200.

George Bush speech at West Point, quoted by Robert L. Bartley, *Wall Street Journal Europe*, September 8, 2003.

CHAPTER 3: THE OLD ALLIANCE

For an excellent background, see Robert Kagan, *Of Paradise and Power: America and Europe in the New World Order* (New York: Knopf, 2003), and his essay, "Power and Weakness," *Policy Review*, June 2002. I am grateful to Kagan for the ability to draw on this work.

Sam Huntington on United States and Islam, see *Hedgehog Review*, vol. 5, no. 1, Spring 2003, Institute of Advanced Studies in Culture, University of Virginia.

Europe, the United Nations, Bosnia, and Rwanda in the 1990s, see Shawcross, op. cit.

Claudio Veliz on French and German leadership of Europe, see *Hedgehog Review*, op. cit.

Andrew Sullivan on the threat of European integration, *New Republic*, June 16, 2003.

John Lloyd on anti-Americanism in Europe, *Financial Times*, February 1–2, 2003. See also John Lloyd's excellent pamphlet, "Iraq and World Order," Foreign Policy Centre, London, 2002.

Chirac and Saddam Hussein, see, for example, Coughlin, op. cit., and Pollack, op. cit.

"Notre Allie Saddam," quoted by Melana Zyla Vickers, in "Saddam's French Connection," *Weekly Standard*, March 10, 2003.

France's Muslim community, see Michael Gonzalez, *Wall Street Journal Europe*, July 2, 2003; see also Simon Kuper, *Financial Times Magazine*, September 27, 2003.

Jack Straw on Chirac "off the leash," Michael Cockerell, "Affairs with the French," BBC 2, September 14, 2003, and *Sunday Times*, September 14, 2003.

Amity Shlaes on German attitudes, *Financial Times Magazine*, May 10, 2003.

Jeffrey Gedmin on Schroeder's campaign against Washington, *Wall Street Journal Europe*, September 23, 2002; on German anti-Americanism, *Weekly Standard*, April 21, 2003. See also Andrew Gimson, *Spectator*, September 13, 2003.

Bush's failure to congratulate Schroeder, *Financial Times*, May 27, 2003.

CHAPTER 4: THE COLLAPSE OF CONSENSUS

European intellectuals' anti-Americanism, John Lloyd, *Financial Times*, February 1–2, 2003.

Amnesty International criticisms of U.S. and UK governments, see Michael Gove, *The Times* (London), December 3, 2002. The secretary-general of Amnesty, Irene Khan, said, "This selective attention to human rights is nothing but a cold and calculated manipulation of the work of human rights activists."

Responsibility to protect, criticism of Blair over warning that war could increase terror, *Financial Times*, September 12, 2003.

United Nations debate, see the excellent series in *Financial Times*, May 27–30, 2003, and *Newsweek*, May 26, 2003.

Robert Kaplan on new Europe, see *Hedgehog Review*, op. cit.

France's real views on WMD: At the February 5 Security Council meeting where Colin Powell presented his dossier on Iraq, Villepin said that "right now, our attention has to be focused as a priority on the biological and chemical domains. It is there that our presumptions about Iraq are the most significant. Regarding the chemical domain, we have evidence of its capacity to produce VX and yperite. In the biological domain, the evidence suggests possible possession of significant stocks of anthrax and botulism toxin, and possibly a production capability. Today the absence of long-range delivery systems reduces the potential threat of these weapons, but we have disturbing signs of Iraq's continued determination to acquire ballistic missiles beyond the authorized 150-kilometer range. In the nuclear domain, we must clarify in particular any attempt by Iraq to acquire aluminium tubes."

Blix's view on inspections. On March 7 Blix said that "even with a proactive Iraqi attitude, induced by continued outside pressure, it would still take some time to verify sites and items. . . and draw conclusions. It would not take years, nor weeks, but months. Neither governments nor inspectors would want disarmament inspection to go on forever. However, . . . a sustained inspection and monitoring system is to remain in place after verified disarmament to give confidence and to strike an alarm, if signs were seen of the revival of any proscribed weapons programmes."

Vaclav Havel, Adam Michnik, and Jose Ramos Horta on the West and Iraqi liberation, quoted by Ian Buruma, *Financial Times Magazine*, September 13, 2003.

CHAPTER 5: THE OZYMANDIAS MOMENT

Eliot Cohen, "How a War Makes Fools of Experts," *Financial Times*, May 12, 2003.

Jay Garner's views, PBS *Frontline*, "Truth, War, and Consequences," aired October 11, 2003.

Carney's views, *Washington Post*, June 22, 2002, and interview with author, June 19 and 21, 2003.

Romano Prodi on European Union and America, *Economist,* April 26, 2003.

Iraqi oil, *Financial Times,* May 23, 2003.

Guardian front-page story, "Straw, Powell Had Serious Doubts Over Their Iraq Weapons Claims: Secret Transcript Revealed," May 31, 2003; correction on page 25, June 5, 2003.

Margaret Drabble on America, *Daily Telegraph* (London), May 8, 2003; David Hare, *Guardian.* June 23, 2003; Andre Glucksman, *Wall Street Journal Europe,* April 28, 2003.

John Burns on journalists in Baghdad, Jack Schafer, SLATE.com, September 24, 2003.

Ian Buruma on America and quoting Gore Vidal, Tariq Ali, *Financial Times Magazine,* September 13, 2003.

Kay report, www.cia.gov.

Rolf Ekeus on missing WMD and on Kay report, *Washington Post,* June 29, 2003, and *Sunday Times* (London), October 19, 2003. Rolf Ekeus wrote of the Kay report, "As a former inspector I was impressed by some of the findings, especially on biological weapons (BW) programmes. Kay convincingly demonstrates that Iraq's biological weapons experts developed and maintained a clandestine network of laboratories and facilities within the security apparatus. None of this was reported earlier this year in Iraq's declaration to the second UN inspection team, Unmovic—an obvious violation of Iraq's reporting obligations. . . . It is difficult to believe that that, had there not been a war, it would have been possible to control and monitor Iraq's dual-use capabilities for any length of time."

Bernard Kerik on setting up a police force in Baghdad, *Wall Street Journal Europe*.

Signs of success in Iraq, see, inter alia, Josh Chafetz, *Weekly Standard*, July 7–14, 2003; Tim Hames, *The Times* (London), August 25, 2003; Vivienne Walt, *Washington Post*, October 3, 2003.

Marsh Arabs get back their water, Rajiv Chandrasekaran, *Washington Post*, October 11, 2003.

De Villepin's attack on United States, The Times (London), September 12, 2003.

Tom Friedman on United States and France "at war," *International Herald Tribune*, September 19, 2003.

London *Times* on France's diplomacy, September 13, 2003.

Fouad Ajami on Arab political class, *Wall Street Journal Europe*, August 26, 2003.

Islamic extremists in Iraq, Michael R. Gordon, *New York Times*, August 10, 2003.

Timetable for handover from United States to Iraqis, Noah Feldman, *New York Times*, September 24, 2003.

CHAPTER 6: THE RIGHT THING TO DO

UN in the new world, see Bill Spindle, *Wall Street Journal Europe*, August 22–24, 2003.

Islamic extremist threats, June 12, 2003, http://memri.org/bin/articles; *Newsweek*, September 8, 2003.

Muslims have a right to kill 4 million, www.worldnetdaily.com, June 12, 2003.

Fouad Ajami on Arab states and American soldiers, *Wall Street Journal Europe*, August 26, 2003.

Kanan Makiya views, PBS *Frontline*, broadcast October 9, 2003.

Opinion polls in Iraq, see, for example, *Spectator* (London), July 19, 2003. This Yougov poll showed that only 7 percent of those questioned wanted Saddam back; 43 percent expected life to be better in a year's time versus 16 percent who did not. In five years time, 54 percent expected it to be better, as against 11 percent who did not. Only 13 percent wanted the American and British troops to leave immediately.

In August a poll conducted by Zogby International for the American Enterprise Institute in four cities showed that seven out of ten expected their lives will be better in five years , and 32 percent said things will be much better. Five out of ten were nervous that democracy could not work in Iraq; 37 percent said they would like their new government modelled on the U.S. system—more than any other state. Only 33 percent wanted an Islamic government; 60 percent said otherwise. Also, 74 percent said Baath Party leaders should be punished, not forgiven. These and other figures seemed to show that the country wanted to move away from the Saddam era and that it was manageable. See Karl Zinsmeister, *Wall Street Journal Europe*, September 10, 2003.

ACKNOWLEDGMENTS

This book began as the Harkness Lecture, delivered at King's College, London, on March 27, 2003. I am very grateful to Peter Osnos of PublicAffairs for suggesting that it should be turned into a short book, to Clive Priddle, an editor with extraordinary skill and patience, for seeing it to completion, and the staff of PublicAffairs.

In London I was helped in the research by Catherine Blyth and by Delphine Jaudeau. I am grateful also to the team of Atlantic Books, including Toby Mundy, Bonnie Chiang, Clare Pierotti, and Valerie Duff.

INDEX

Suez Canal, 76
Sullivan, Andrew, 88
Svoboda, Cyril, 129
Swinging six, 142
Syria
    neocons and, 58
    post-war support of, 172

Taliban, 64, 85
    regrouping of, 227
    U.S. attack on, 90
Terrorist act(s)
    al-Hashemi assassination, 198
    Al Rashid Hotel, 227
    Baqir assassination, 198
    Canal Hotel (UN), 1–2, 5–7, 197
    Jordanian embassy, 197
    9/11, 1, 11–14
    Red Cross, 227–228
    Teheran U.S. Embassy, 20
    unconventional weapons in, 14
    U.S. helicopter, 228
Thatcher, Margaret, 39, 45, 219
    German reunification and, 101
    Kuwait invasion and, 22
The Third Way, 46
The Threatening Storm: The Case for
    Invading Iraq (Pollack), 97, 152
Total/Fina/Elf, 97
Trotskyist movement, 62
Truman, Harry, 68

Uni-multipolar system, 78
UNICEF, 141

United Nations Development Pro-
    gramme, 15, 231
United Nations Special Commis-
    sion on Iraq. See UNSCOM
United Nations (UN). See also
    UNMOVIC; UNSCOM
    Article 51 and, 114
    Bush speech to, 110
    Canal Hotel bombing of, 1–2
    changes necessary in, 219–220
    Iraq and attack on, 1–2, 5–6, 197
    Iraq changeover and, 205–206,
        210
    Iraq sanctions by, 26, 29–30, 34
    Iraq withdrawal by, 197
    Kosovo action and, 83–85
    neocon criticisms of, 58–59
    oil-for-food program in, 29–30,
        33
    oil sanctions by, 26, 29–30, 34–35
    preemptive doctrine and, 69
    relevance of, 139–140, 214
    Resolution 678 by, 22, 113–114,
        118
    Resolution 687 by, 26–27, 113
    Resolution 1134 by, 30
    Resolution 1284 by, 33–34, 114
    Resolution 1441 by, 116–119, 121,
        134, 149, 153, 187, 193
    Resolution 1483 by, 4, 175–176,
        178–179
    Resolution 1551 by, 211–212
    resolution requirement by,
        141–146, 149
    responsibilities of, 81
    swinging six and, 142

PublicAffairs is a publishing house founded in 1997. It is a tribute to the standards, values, and flair of three persons who have served as mentors to countless reporters, writers, editors, and book people of all kinds, including me.

I.F. STONE, proprietor of *I. F. Stone's Weekly*, combined a commitment to the First Amendment with entrepreneurial zeal and reporting skill and became one of the great independent journalists in American history. At the age of eighty, Izzy published *The Trial of Socrates*, which was a national bestseller. He wrote the book after he taught himself ancient Greek.

BENJAMIN C. BRADLEE was for nearly thirty years the charismatic editorial leader of *The Washington Post*. It was Ben who gave the *Post* the range and courage to pursue such historic issues as Watergate. He supported his reporters with a tenacity that made them fearless and it is no accident that so many became authors of influential, best-selling books.

ROBERT L. BERNSTEIN, the chief executive of Random House for more than a quarter century, guided one of the nation's premier publishing houses. Bob was personally responsible for many books of political dissent and argument that challenged tyranny around the globe. He is also the founder and longtime chair of Human Rights Watch, one of the most respected human rights organizations in the world.

For fifty years, the banner of Public Affairs Press was carried by its owner Morris B. Schnapper, who published Gandhi, Nasser, Toynbee, Truman, and about 1,500 other authors. In 1983, Schnapper was described by *The Washington Post* as "a redoubtable gadfly." His legacy will endure in the books to come.

Peter Osnos, *Publisher*